JAMES McNAIR

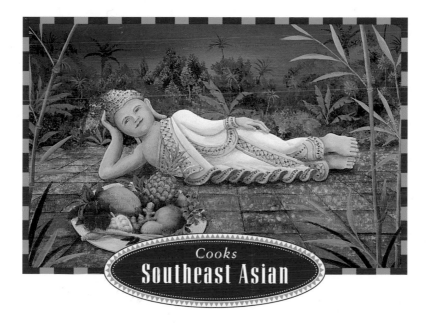

Cooks
Southeast Asian

PHOTOGRAPHY AND STYLING BY JAMES McNAIR

CHRONICLE BOOKS
SAN FRANCISCO

Printed in Hong Kong.

Library of Congress Cataloging-in-Publication Data available

ISBN 0-8118-0453-4 (PBK)
ISBN 0-8118-0483-6 (HC)

Distributed in Canada by
Raincoast Books
8680 Cambie Street
Vancouver, British Columbia V6P 6M9

10 9 8 7 6 5 4 3 2 1

Chronicle Books
275 Fifth Street
San Francisco, California 94103

For Naila Gallagher, a good friend, fabulous cook, and loving auntie, who shares her pearls of wisdom, gives terrific haircuts, and enjoys all things exotic.

And in memory of my tropical bird, Dweasel Pickle, who sat alongside my desk or on my shoulder throughout the writing of seventeen cookbooks and for much of this volume. My world is much quieter without my dear little friend.

Editorial and Photographic Production by James McNair and Andrew Moore
Villa Sunshine Books, Napa Valley, California.

Book Design and Typography by Rick Dinihanian and John Lyle
Green Lizard Design, St. Helena, California.

Many of the dishes, glassware, flatware, linens, and accessories in the photographs are from Fillamento, San Francisco.

The author as a Thai dancer on the back cover and the portrait of Dweasel on this page were painted by Alan May.

The title page illustration and the background on pages 8 and 9 were painted by Michael Duté.

CONTENTS

Southeast Asia remains among the most exotic and intriguing regions on the planet. Although several of the countries in the area are developing at an unprecedented pace, their steamy jungles, spectacular beaches, and teeming cities that predate European capitals remain shrouded in mystery to much of the rest of the world.

The foods of these ancient cultures look and taste exotic to most North Americans, but I've yet to find a single person who hasn't succumbed to their seductive tropical lure. When thinking about the dishes of the region, two words come to mind: *fresh* and *explosive*. No other cuisines on earth seem to feature such fresh ingredients that explode with such contrasting flavors. One bite may incorporate tart lime, tangy lemongrass, sour tamarind, salty fish sauce, fiery chile, and sweet palm sugar, all made even more lively with pungent cilantro or zesty mint. Likewise, the melange of textures ranges from crunchy peanuts to satiny rice noodles to velvety coconut milk.

The cuisines of this region, which have been influenced over the centuries by their Chinese, Indian, Portuguese, Dutch, and British rulers, settlers, and neighbors, have become a passion for me since I first discovered them some years ago. I've now made room on my culinary pedestal for these exquisite delicacies.

This book features a collection of my own favorite dishes gleaned over the years from travels, books and magazines, restaurants, good home cooks and fellow food professionals who've lived in Southeast Asia, and my own kitchen experiments. A volume of this size certainly cannot pretend to be a definitive book on the cooking of this vast and varied region of the world. What I am offering here is my own interpretation of some classic dishes of the region, written so that they might be prepared in any home kitchen. I admit to the absence of certain popular Southeast Asian dishes in this volume, including my favorite recipes from the Philippines, as many have already been published in my single-subject book series. For your convenience, an index to those recipes is included on page 163.

Like many other residents of the San Francisco Bay Area, I consider myself fortunate to live within a short drive of what are reputed to be some of the best Southeast Asian restaurants on either side of the Pacific. On a typical day I might dine on a Vietnamese lunch at Le Soleil or The Golden Turtle in San Francisco, then transport myself to Indonesia by sitting down to an exquisite dinner at The Rice Table in nearby San Rafael. A visit to San Francisco's Richmond district allows me to choose from Burmese fare at Mandalay, Cambodian cuisine at Angkor Wat, Malaysian dishes at Singapore Malaysia, or the varied cooking of Singapore at Straits Cafe. Often, I opt for a return visit to Swatdee in the city's Noe Valley for my favorite Thai specialties, or I try another one of the seemingly countless Thai establishments that dot the streets of San Francisco.

Not only will this book make it possible for you to cook this exotic fare at home, but it will also prove helpful in deciphering menus when dining out in Southeast Asian restaurants at home or abroad.

Join me now in an exciting cook's tour through Southeast Asia, with stops in Myanmar (Burma), Thailand, Laos, Cambodia, Vietnam, Malaysia, Singapore, and Indonesia. En route, you'll sample some of the most appealing foods on earth.

Breakfast throughout these warm-weather nations may be anything left over from the previous day, a bowl of noodles or rice porridge with a variety of toppings (page 20), or a hot soup. The other two meals of the day center around rice in some form accompanied by one, a few, or many other dishes. Sweets are normally consumed as snacks between meals.

Southeast Asian meals offer contrasts in flavors, temperatures, and textures. There is usually something spicy as well as soothing, salty as well as sweet, warm as well as cool, smooth as well as crunchy. And when the weather is exceptionally hot, the evening meal sometimes consists of only rice.

Tables, elevated woven trays, or mats on the floor are set with individual dinner plates, forks, and spoons; the forks are used to push the food on the plate into the spoon for eating. Knives are unnecessary since the food is usually cut into small pieces before cooking or can easily be broken up with the fork and spoon. If soup will be served, small individual bowls and Chinese-style porcelain spoons or spoons carved from coconut shells may be provided for each diner. In Vietnam and in Chinese communities scattered throughout the region, chopsticks replace forks and spoons and bowls commonly replace the flat plates that are favored elsewhere. Noodle dishes throughout the area, however, are often eaten with chopsticks, as they are thought of as Chinese food.

It is still considered polite in some circles to eat with the fingertips of the right hand, a centuries-old practice. When meals are served in this manner, fingerbowls of water and lime slices are provided for each diner, or hot water with soap and towels are offered at the table before the fruit or sweet is served.

With the exception of rice, all finished dishes are served hot, warm, or at room temperature. Many preparations, such as curries, are made ahead and are then gently reheated while the rice is cooking. Generally, each of the dishes is cooked and placed on the table along with condiments and accompaniments. Then, when the perfectly cooked rice is ready, it is brought to the table and the meal begins.

Southeast Asians do not follow the Western pattern of eating in courses. Except for fruits or desserts, all dishes, including soups and salads, are placed on the table at the same time. Each diner scoops a modest serving of rice onto the center of a plate or bowl and then surrounds it with small servings of the other dishes and condiments. It is considered rude to load up plates with large Western-sized servings at the beginning of the meal, but it is certainly acceptable to have several helpings of the dishes. When soups are included, they are ladled into individual bowls and eaten a few sips at a time throughout the meal. Exceptions include full-meal soups, such as Vietnamese *pho* or Indonesian and Malaysian *soto ayam*, which are served to diners in large bowls.

The Southeast Asian pantry includes a variety of condiments and seasonings served in small containers that allow diners to adjust the flavor of each dish to suit their own taste. Tables throughout the region commonly hold some sort of chile sauce or fresh chiles. Additional offerings may include chopped peanuts, dried shrimp, cooling cucumbers, lime wedges, fresh herbs, and bottles of fish sauce. In Indonesia and Malaysia, containers of sweet soy sauce, or *kecap manis*, are ubiquitous.

Fresh fruit or sweetened cold drinks are offered to conclude daily meals and help tame the savage heat. Fancier desserts are normally reserved for special occasions.

Water is the most popular mealtime drink, and certainly one of the most thirst-quenching foils to spicy fare. Other cooling beverages include lime- and ginger-based drinks and concoctions made from coconut milk. Beer is a popular antidote to the tropical heat, but it will actually magnify the heat of chile-laden dishes. Rice wine is sipped from time to time. If you wish to match other wines with these fiery fares, fruity whites such as Chenin Blanc, Gewürztraminer, Riesling, or white Zinfandel or other blushes are generally best. Contemporary Southeast Asian professionals enjoy spirits and a bottle is likely to be placed on the table for sipping throughout a business meal.

Unlike the custom in some other Asian cultures, hot tea is not served throughout the meal. Fruit or sweets may be accompanied by a cup of hot tea or robust coffee, or exotically spiced iced tea or coffee may take the place of another sweet ending.

RECIPES

Southeast Asian dishes vary according to the taste of local cooks, who rarely follow written recipes. In keeping with that spirit and my own philosophy of cooking, I offer my recipes as a point of departure for your own innovation. They establish my style for each dish and I encourage you to prepare them exactly as written the first time to experience the balance of flavors that I prefer. The second time, feel free to adapt the seasonings to suit your own palate.

To help with learning about ingredients that are unique to Southeast Asia, including coconut milk, fish sauce, galanga, lemongrass, and palm sugar, a shopping guide has been included on pages 160-162. There you'll also find clues for where to shop and any acceptable substitutions that can be made for the ingredients. If you are not familiar with Southeast Asian cooking, I suggest a thorough reading of this guide before beginning to use the recipes.

For those Southeast Asian languages using writing systems different from our own, the original language recipe titles and ingredient names have been transliterated into our Latin alphabet. Do not be surprised if these spellings differ from those you have seen on Southeast Asian menus or in other books, as English equivalent spellings regularly vary from source to source. I have also not included the various diacritical marks used with Vietnamese words.

And since Southeast Asian meals do not follow our usual appetizer through dessert sequence, I have not divided my recipes into the familiar chapters of Western cookbooks. I have, however, placed the recipes in an order that is useful in menu planning, beginning with beverages that may be served before or along with the meal and ending with sweet dishes that are traditionally served as snacks or special-occasion desserts following a meal. In between, I've adhered to the following order: rice and dishes made with rice, noodle dishes and soups that contain noodles, then vegetable dishes, followed by fish, poultry, and meats.

The number of servings that I have specified for each recipe is based on the Southeast Asian practice of offering several dishes together with diners taking small portions of each. If you wish to serve fewer dishes, consider doubling or tripling a recipe.

NAHM MENOW AND NAHM KING
...
Thai

LIMEADE AND GINGER DRINKS

In the steamy climate of Thailand, the bountiful limes are turned into a thirst-quenching limeade, or nahm menow. A generous amount of salt traditionally seasons this drink; I prefer only a small portion, but feel free to add more or omit it altogether. For an unusual gingered limeade variation, substitute Ginger Syrup (page 153) for the Simple Sugar Syrup.

Neither of the throat-tingling ginger-based treats is an authentic Southeast Asian beverage. They were developed by Andrew Moore during our work on this book and are definitely in the spirit of the area. ❧

10

LIMEADE
1 cup Simple Sugar Syrup (page 153)
½ cup freshly squeezed lime juice
6 cups water
¼ teaspoon salt
Ice cubes
Lime slices
Fresh mint sprigs

Prepare the Simple Sugar Syrup as directed, then cover and refrigerate until chilled.

In a large pitcher, combine the Simple Sugar Syrup, lime juice, water, and salt. Cover tightly and refrigerate until well chilled.

Fill tall glasses with ice cubes, lime slices, and mint sprigs, then fill with the chilled limeade. Serve immediately.

Makes 6 servings.

GINGER SODA
¼ cup Ginger Syrup (page 153)
¾ cup sparkling water or club soda
Ice cubes or crushed ice
Fresh mint sprigs for garnish (optional)

Prepare the Ginger Syrup as directed, then cover and refrigerate until chilled.

In a tall glass, combine the Ginger Syrup and sparkling water or soda and stir to blend. Add ice, garnish with mint sprigs (if using), and serve immediately.

Makes 1 serving.

BANGKOKTAIL
1 ounce (2 tablespoons) Ginger Syrup (page 153)
1 ounce (2 tablespoons) light rum
¾ ounce (1½ tablespoons) freshly squeezed lime juice
Ice cubes
Lime slice or twist for garnish

Prepare the Ginger Syrup as directed, then cover and refrigerate until chilled.

In a cocktail shaker, combine the Ginger Syrup, rum, and lime juice. Shake, then strain into a tumbler. Add ice, garnish with a lime slice or twist, and serve immediately.

Makes 1 serving.

CHA YEN THAI
Thai

THAI ICED TEA

*E*ven though Thais normally enjoy
this unusual drink after or between
meals, I find it a delightful before-
meal beverage or anytime pick-me-
up and always make a double or
triple amount.

Thais prefer their tea very sweet.
Although I've reduced the customary
sweetness a bit, you may wish to cut
the sweetener even more. Add either
simple syrup or canned sweetened
condensed milk to the tea before
chilling; the condensed milk creates a
peach tint, while the syrup doesn't
change the tea's brick-orange hue.

The creamy crown on each serving
is traditionally canned milk, used
because of the scarcity of fresh dairy
products. It also adds a richer flavor
than fresh half-and-half. ◖

THAI ICED TEA

Thai tea (*cha Thai*) is a blend of finely chopped black tea leaves, vanilla bean, ground sweet spices such as cinnamon and star anise, and orange food coloring. Do not attempt to make this refreshing drink with any other tea.

1½ cups Simple Sugar Syrup (page 153), or to taste, or 1 can (14 ounces)
  sweetened condensed milk, or to taste
5 cups water
1 cup Thai tea leaves (*cha Thai*; see recipe introduction above)
Ice cubes or crushed ice
1 to 1½ cups evaporated milk or half-and-half

If using Simple Sugar Syrup, prepare as directed and set aside. If using condensed milk, reserve for later use.

In a saucepan or kettle, bring the water to a rapid boil. Remove from the heat, stir in the tea leaves, and let steep for 3 to 4 minutes. Or place the tea in a teapot, add the boiling water, stir well, and let steep.

Position a fine-mesh sieve over a large heat-resistant pitcher and strain the steeped tea into the pitcher. Set the sieve over the original container and pour the liquid from the pitcher back over the tea leaves. Repeat this procedure 5 or 6 times until the tea is strong and a deep terra-cotta.

Strain the tea through a coffee filter into a pitcher to remove any fine dregs. Sweeten with the simple syrup or condensed milk, stirring to blend well; the warm tea should taste sweeter than you wish, to allow for chilling and dilution with milk. Let cool to room temperature, then cover tightly and refrigerate until chilled, at least 1 hour or for up to 5 days.

To serve, fill tall glasses with ice, then pour in enough chilled tea to fill each glass about three-fourths full. Pour about ¼ cup evaporated milk or half-and-half over the top of each glass and serve immediately.

Makes 6 servings.

SOUTHEAST ASIAN COFFEE

THAI COFFEE
1½ cups Simple Sugar Syrup (page 153), or to taste, or 1 can (14 ounces)
   sweetened condensed milk, or to taste
4 cups water
¼ cup Thai coffee powder (see recipe introduction)
1 to 1½ cups evaporated milk or half-and-half
Ice cubes or crushed ice, if serving cold

If using Simple Sugar Syrup, prepare as directed and set aside. If using condensed milk, reserve for later use.

In a deep saucepan, bring the water to a boil over medium-high heat. Stir in the coffee powder and return to a boil. Remove the pan from the heat and set aside to steep for a few minutes.

Strain the coffee through a coffee filter into a serving pot or heat-resistant pitcher. Sweeten with the simple syrup or condensed milk, stirring to blend well.

To serve hot, pour the coffee into tall heat-resistant glasses. Pour about ¼ cup evaporated milk or half-and-half over the top of each glass.

To serve cold, let the sweetened coffee cool to room temperature, then cover tightly and refrigerate until chilled, at least 1 hour or for up to 5 days. Fill tall glasses with ice, then pour in enough chilled coffee to fill each glass about three-fourths full. Pour about ¼ cup evaporated milk or half-and-half over the top of each glass and serve immediately.

Makes 4 to 6 servings.

VIETNAMESE COFFEE
¼ to ½ cup sweetened condensed milk
2 to 3 cups hot, strongly brewed French-roast coffee
Ice cubes, if serving cold

To serve hot, pour the condensed milk to taste in the bottom of four 8-ounce clear heat-resistant glasses. Slowly pour in the coffee, being careful not to disturb the layer of milk. Serve immediately. The milk is stirred into the coffee before drinking. (To use an individual drip pot, position it over the glass, add about 2 tablespoons ground coffee, and then slowly pour in about ¾ cup boiling water.)

To serve cold, pour the condensed milk into tall glasses, fill with ice cubes, add the coffee, and serve immediately. (If using individual drip pots, drip the coffee into the milk as described above, stir well, and then pour the mixture over ice in a separate glass.)

Makes 4 servings.

CAPHE
...
Vietnamese

KAH-FE
...
Thai

SOUTHEAST ASIAN COFFEE

Thais combine coffee beans with roasted sesame seeds and corn and grind the mixture to a powder. In Asian markets look for bags labeled oliang or Thai coffee (kah-fe). The mixture is brewed strong, heavily sweetened, and mellowed with milk.

Vietnamese and Cambodians prefer plain dark-roasted coffee (caphe in Vietnamese) and often slowly drip it through special individual pots set directly over glasses containing sweetened condensed milk; it is frequently drunk over ice. The rest of Southeast Asia serves strong brewed coffee with milk and sugar. Coffee beans from Java and Sumatra are prized by coffee lovers everywhere. ❧

ARROZ
...
Filipino

COM
...
Vietnamese

HTAMIN
...
Burmese

KAO
...
Thai

NASI
...
Indonesian and Malaysian

POUN
...
Cambodian

RICE

*A*lthough the type of grain may

vary, Southeast Asians build every

meal around generous portions of rice.

In Indonesia, Malaysia, Myanmar

(Burma), Thailand, and Vietnam,

long-grain rice kernels of indica

varieties are the daily choice and

many types are available there that

are not exported. When properly

cooked, these slim grains are

somewhat firm and remain slightly

separated. In Cambodia and the

Philippines, medium- or short-grain

varieties are the choice; they render

RICE

WHITE RICE

Jasmine (sometimes spelled jasmin) rice *(kao hohm mali)* from Thailand, a long-grain variety with a nutty aroma and subtle flavor, is my favorite rice and was used in developing this recipe. A delicious alternative is basmati rice, a slender, long-grain, highly aromatic rice that originated in India but is now also grown in the United States. Regular American-grown rice from the supermarket can be used if these flavorful varieties are unavailable. Although perfectly fine for some other purposes, please do not consider parboiled (trademarked as Converted) rice for Southeast Asian dining; the grains do not cling when cooked, making the rice inappropriate for these tropical cuisines.

The exact amount of liquid and cooking time may vary with the type of rice, length of storage, altitude, and personal preference. Initially, use the measurements given, then adjust the amount of liquid and/or cooking time if necessary for future pots of rice.

2 cups white rice (see recipe introduction above for types)
3 cups water

If using imported rice, spread it out on a tray or flat surface and pick over it by hand to remove any foreign bits or imperfect grains. Place the rice in a bowl and add water to cover. Stir vigorously with your fingertips, then drain off the water. Repeat this procedure several times until the water runs almost clear. (For more uniformly cooked rice, add fresh water to cover completely, and soak for about 1 hour. Drain just before cooking.)

To cook in a heavy saucepan, combine the rice and water and place over medium-high heat. Bring to a boil, then stir once, reduce the heat to very low, cover tightly, and cook for 17 minutes. Do not remove the cover or stir during cooking. Remove the rice from the heat and remove the lid briefly to check the rice. (If any liquid remains in the pot, cover again and place over low heat until the liquid evaporates, 2 to 4 minutes, then remove from the heat.) Replace the cover and let stand undisturbed for 10 minutes.

To cook in a rice cooker, combine the rice and water in the insert pan, cover with the lid, and turn on. Let stand for about 10 minutes after the appliance shuts off.

Remove the lid from the pan or rice cooker and fluff the rice with a fork, lifting from the bottom instead of stirring, to separate the grains gently. Serve warm.

Makes about 6 cups; enough for 4 to 6 servings.

WHITE RICE VARIATIONS

Chicken Rice. Substitute homemade chicken stock or canned reduced-sodium chicken broth for the water.

Coconut Rice. Omit the water, and in its place use Fresh Coconut Milk, Medium Variation (page 141) or 2 cups shaken canned coconut milk diluted with 1 cup water.

Recipe continues on page 18

cooked grains that are softer and cling together, although they remain individually defined. Long-, medium-, or short-grained rice may all be cooked as described in the recipe for White Rice. Glutinous rice is favored in Laos and northwest Thailand and directions for cooking it are given in the recipe for Sticky Rice.

Along with many Southeast Asian cooks, I prefer to wash rice to remove the miller's dusting of starch or talc, although rice packers say that this step is unnecessary.

The recipe for White Rice cooks rice by the absorption method, allowing the grains to absorb all of the liquid in the pot; this is usually referred to erroneously as steamed rice. When cooking larger amounts of rice, use the following general rule: 3 cups liquid for the first 2 cups of rice, then add only 1 cup liquid for each additional cup of grain.

Malaysian-Style Coconut Rice (*nasi lemak*). Use coconut milk in place of the water as described above. Using the tines of a fork, scrape 2 fresh or thawed frozen screwpine (*pandan*) leaves to release their flavor, then tie the leaves into knots and add them to the top of the rice before cooking; discard the leaves once the rice is done.

Ginger Rice. Add ¼ cup minced or grated fresh ginger to the cooking water or to an equal amount of homemade chicken stock or canned reduced-sodium chicken broth. Alternatively, wrap ½ cup finely chopped fresh ginger in cheesecloth and squeeze to release the juice into a measuring cup. Then add water, stock, or broth to equal 3 cups for cooking the rice.

STICKY RICE

Also called glutinous, sweet, or waxy rice, sticky rice is the daily grain of preference in Laos and northeast Thailand. Elsewhere in the region it is used to make sweets or snacks and ceremonial foods. The use of the word sticky does not come from the rice being overcooked; it instead refers to rice varieties that cling together naturally during cooking and are sweeter and stronger in flavor than other rice varieties. Although called sweet, the rice is not distinctively sweeter than *indica* rice; the name comes from its use in making sweet dishes.

Asian markets carry imported sticky rice in white, brown, or black; the dark varieties are usually reserved for sweet dishes, but the white rice may accompany savory dishes or be used in the making of sweets. Plan ahead, as the grains must be soaked prior to cooking. Cooking time will vary according to length of soaking.

2 cups white, brown, or black glutinous rice

Spread the rice out on a tray or flat surface and pick over it by hand to remove any foreign bits or imperfect grains. Place the rice in a bowl and add cold water to cover. Stir vigorously with your fingertips, then drain off the water. Repeat this procedure several times until the water runs almost clear. Drain the rice, add enough fresh water to cover completely, and let soak for at least 4 hours or, preferably, overnight.

To prepare for steaming, position a rack in a wok or pan that will be large enough to hold a steamer basket or colander and can be completely covered by a lid. Pour in water to a level just below the steaming rack and place over high heat. Bring to a boil, then lower the heat to achieve a simmer.

If using a steamer basket or colander with holes that are large enough to allow the rice to fall through, line the steamer basket or colander with several layers of moistened cheesecloth or a piece of banana leaf. Drain the rice and spread it evenly in the prepared container. Transfer to the steamer rack over the simmering water, making sure that the rice does not come in contact with the water. Cover the wok or pan tightly and steam until the rice is tender, 25 to 35 minutes for white rice, or about 1 hour for brown or black rice Adjust the heat to maintain simmering water and continuous steam throughout cooking, adding boiling water if needed to maintain water level. For softer rice, sprinkle about ¼ cup water over the top of the rice 2 or 3 times during steaming.

Remove the rice from the steamer and transfer to a serving container. Serve warm or at room temperature, or use as directed in recipes. Do not refrigerate, as it will turn into a gooey mass.

Makes about 4 cups, enough for 4 servings.

STICKY RICE VARIATIONS
Coconut Sticky Rice. Place the drained soaked rice in a pot with 3 cups Fresh Coconut Milk, Medium Variation (page 141) or 2 cups shaken canned coconut milk diluted with 1 cup water. (If cooking more than 2 cups of rice, add only 1 cup coconut milk for each additional cup of rice.) Bring to a boil over high heat. Reduce the heat to very low, cover tightly, and cook until the rice is tender and liquid has evaporated, about 15 minutes for white rice, or 35 to 45 minutes for brown or black rice. Remove from the heat and let stand, covered, for 15 minutes.

Sweet Sticky Rice. Cook sticky rice as directed in the recipe. In a saucepan, combine 1¾ cups Fresh Coconut Milk (page 140) or shaken canned coconut milk, ⅔ cup palm sugar, and ½ teaspoon salt and stir over medium-high heat until the sugar is dissolved, about 3 minutes. Pour over the warm rice in a mixing bowl, stir to combine, and let stand, uncovered, for 30 minutes. Serve with ripe mangoes or other fresh fruit.

Except in Myanmar, rice is never salted or cooked in stock, as the rice is always eaten with dishes that contain plenty of flavor.

If you cook rice frequently and have room for another kitchen appliance, you might wish to invest in an electric rice cooker, which consistently produces perfect white rice and is now commonplace in many Southeast Asian kitchens. Rice cookers should not be used when cooking sticky rice.

Southeast Asian markets sell special woven baskets with straw lids for steaming sticky rice, which is generally served directly from the basket. The rice is normally eaten by pinching off small portions with one hand and rolling it into a ball before popping it into the mouth, often times after first dipping it into a sauce or combining it with fruit or other food. ❧

KAO TOME
...
Thai

RICE PORRIDGE

*I*mmigrants from China spread their rice porridge, or jook, throughout much of Southeast Asia, where it became a breakfast dish as well as a late-night treat. The bland rice, called congee by English-speaking residents in the region, gets its flavor from a variety of toppings.

For a thinner porridge, add more water; for a thicker version, reduce the amount of water. You can also start the porridge with leftover cooked rice, using twice as much liquid as rice. ❧

RICE PORRIDGE

½ cup long-, medium-, or short-grain white rice
5 cups homemade light chicken stock or water, or 3 cups canned
   reduced-sodium chicken broth diluted with 2 cups water

TOPPINGS
Omelet Strips (page 156)
Fried Shallot (page 157)
Pickled Garlic (page 155)
Pickled Ginger (page 154)
Sweet Chile-Garlic Dipping Sauce (page 146)
Sweet Soy Sauce (page 149) or bottled Indonesian sweet soy sauce
   (*kecap manis*)
Red Chile Sauce (page 148) or bottled red chile sauce (Indonesian
   sambal ulek or Vietnamese *tuong ot*)
Dried or cooked shrimp
Salty Chinese-style pickled vegetables
Hard-cooked eggs, preferably Chinese-style salted duck eggs, sliced
Chopped roasted peanuts
Leftover curry
Stir-fried minced chicken, beef, or pork
Sliced green onion
Minced fresh ginger
Fresh cilantro (coriander) leaves
Fresh Asian basil leaves

Spread the rice out on a tray or flat surface and pick over it by hand to remove any foreign bits or imperfect grains. Place the rice in a bowl and add cold water to cover. Stir vigorously with your fingertips, then drain off the water. Repeat this procedure several times until the water runs almost clear.

In a heavy saucepan, combine the rice and chicken stock, water, or diluted broth. Place over medium-high heat and bring to a boil. Reduce the heat to very low, cover tightly, and simmer, stirring occasionally, until the rice is very soft and creamy, about 2 hours.

Meanwhile, prepare as many of the toppings as desired and place in separate bowls on the table.

To serve, ladle the porridge into individual bowls. Diners sprinkle selected toppings over their servings.

Makes 4 servings.

GOLDEN FESTIVAL RICE

5 cups Fresh Coconut Milk, Thin Variation (page 141), or 2½ cups shaken
   canned coconut milk diluted with 2½ cups water
4 cups long-grain white rice or white glutinous rice
Fried Shallot (page 157)
Shrimp or Prawn Chips (page 69)
2½ teaspoons ground turmeric
1 tablespoon minced garlic
1 screwpine (*pandan*) leaf (optional)
Fresh banana leaf or ti leaves for serving (optional)
3 tablespoons minced fresh chives
3 tablespoons minced red hot chile

If using Fresh Coconut Milk, prepare as directed and set aside. If using canned
coconut milk, reserve for later use.

Spread the rice out on a tray or flat surface and pick over it by hand to remove
any foreign bits or imperfect grains. Place the rice in a bowl and add cold water
to cover. Stir vigorously with your fingertips, then drain off the water. Repeat this
procedure several times until the water runs almost clear. If using long-grain rice,
proceed with cooking. If using glutinous rice, drain the rice, add fresh water to
cover completely, and soak for at least 4 hours or, preferably, overnight.

Meanwhile, prepare the Fried Shallot and Shrimp or Prawn Chips as directed and
set aside separately.

Drain the rice and transfer to a saucepan. Add the coconut milk, turmeric, and
garlic and blend well. Using the tines of a fork, scrape the screwpine leaf (if using)
to release the flavor, tie into a knot, and place in the center of the rice. Place over
medium-high heat and bring to a boil. Stir once, reduce the heat to very low, cover
tightly, and cook until the coconut milk is absorbed, about 15 minutes for long-
grain rice or about 20 minutes for glutinous rice.

Line a serving plate or flat basket with the banana leaf or ti leaves (if using). Discard
the screw-pine leaf (if used) and spoon the rice onto the serving plate or basket to
form a mound. Alternatively, spoon the rice into a buttered 2-quart mold or bowl,
let set for 10 minutes, and then invert onto the serving plate or basket and carefully
pull off the mold or bowl.

Crown the rice with the Fried Shallot, then shower with the chives and chile and
surround with the Shrimp or Prawn Chips. Serve warm or at room temperature.

Makes 8 servings.

NASI KUNING
Indonesian
NASI KUNYIT
Malaysian

GOLDEN FESTIVAL RICE

*A tower of golden glutinous rice
cooked in coconut milk appears on
the tables for festivals and other
special occasions in Singapore and
throughout Malaysia. Indonesians
prepare their version with long-grain
rice that cooks up to a fluffy finish.*

*In addition to the crisp chips, the
finished mound of rice may be
surrounded with curry, sate, fried
chicken, hard-cooked egg slices,
cucumber slices, toasted coconut,
or other favorite additions.* ❧

NASI GORENG
Indonesian and Malaysian

FRIED RICE

*F*rugal Indonesian cooks created
this Chinese-inspired dish to use up
leftover rice, but it's worth making
rice just so that you can put together
this tasty combination.

*As with all stir-fried dishes, have all
the ingredients ready and lined up
alongside the stove before you begin
cooking.*

*Fried noodles (bahmi goreng) can
be made by preparing 12 ounces
dried thin egg or rice noodles as
described on page 159 and using
them in place of the rice.* ❧

24

White Rice (page 16)
Fried Shallot (page 157)
Omelet Strips (page 156)
¼ cup Tamarind Liquid (page 156)
¼ cup Sweet Soy Sauce (page 149) or bottled Indonesian sweet soy sauce
   (*kecap manis*)
1 tablespoon Red Chile Sauce (page 148) or bottled red chile sauce (Indonesian
   sambal ulek or Vietnamese *tuong ot*)
¼ cup canola oil or other high-quality vegetable oil
1½ cups chopped shallot
1 tablespoon minced fresh ginger
2 teaspoons minced or pressed garlic
½ teaspoon crumbled firm dried shrimp paste (Indonesian *trasi* or Malaysian *blachan*)
8 ounces shrimp, peeled, deveined, and coarsely chopped
8 ounces boneless lean pork or beef or boned and skinned chicken breast, cut into
   bite-sized pieces
1½ cups finely shredded cabbage, preferably napa or other Asian variety
1 cup mung bean sprouts
Salt
Freshly ground black pepper
5 tablespoons thinly sliced green onion, including green tops
Fresh celery leaves, preferably Chinese variety (Indonesian *seledri*), for garnish

Cook the rice as directed and set aside to cool. Prepare the Fried Shallot, Omelet Strips,
and Tamarind Liquid as directed and set aside separately.

If using Sweet Soy Sauce and/or Red Chile Sauce, prepare as directed and set each aside.
If using bottled sauces, reserve for later use.

Place a wok, large sauté pan, or large, heavy skillet over medium-high heat. When the pan
is hot, add the oil and swirl to coat the pan. When the oil is hot but not yet smoking, add
the chopped shallot and stir-fry for about 1 minute. Add the ginger, garlic, and shrimp
paste and stir-fry for about 2 minutes longer. Add the shrimp and meat and stir-fry until
the shrimp turn opaque and pink and the meat is just past the pink stage, about 5 minutes
longer. Add the cabbage and bean sprouts and stir-fry just until the cabbage is wilted, about
2 minutes longer. Season to taste with salt and pepper.

Add the rice, green onion, Tamarind Liquid, sweet soy sauce, and chile sauce and stir-fry,
using the cooking implement to break up any rice that clumps together, until the rice is
heated through, about 2 minutes. Taste and adjust the seasonings to achieve a balance of
sour, sweet, salty, and hot.

To serve, mound the rice on a serving plate or basket. Crown with the Fried Shallot and
Omelet Strips and garnish with the celery leaves.

Makes 6 servings.

LEMPER
• • •
Indonesian and Malaysian

STUFFED RICE ROLLS

Good cooks in Indonesia and Malaysia fill these little snacks with a wide variety of freshly made or leftover mixtures, including stir-fried meats or vegetables, curries, grilled sate, tempeh, cooked fish, and fresh or cooked fruits.

If you don't have a banana tree in your backyard, see page 160 for sources or substitutions. ❧

STUFFED RICE ROLLS

Sticky Rice, Coconut Variation (page 19)
Sweet Soy Sauce (page 149) or bottled Indonesian sweet soy sauce (*kecap manis*)

STUFFING
1 tablespoon canola oil or other high-quality vegetable oil
¼ cup minced shallot
4 ounces lean pork or boned and skinned chicken breast, ground or minced
3 tablespoons finely chopped red sweet pepper
3 tablespoons finely chopped carrot
3 tablespoons finely chopped jicama
3 tablespoons finely chopped canned bamboo shoots
1 teaspoon minced or pressed garlic
1 teaspoon sugar
1 teaspoon ground cumin
¼ teaspoon ground turmeric
1 tablespoon soy sauce
Freshly ground black pepper
3 tablespoons minced fresh cilantro (coriander)

5 pieces fresh or thawed frozen banana leaves, tough center spines discarded, then leaf halves cut into 8-by-12-inch rectangles
Boiling water

Cook the rice as directed and set aside to cool. If using Sweet Soy Sauce, prepare as directed and set aside. If using bottled sauce, reserve for later use.

To make the stuffing, place a wok, sauté pan, or heavy skillet over high heat. When the pan is hot, add the oil and swirl to coat the pan. When the oil is hot, add the shallot and stir-fry for about 1 minute. Add the pork or chicken, sweet pepper, carrot, jicama, bamboo shoots, garlic, sugar, cumin, and turmeric and stir-fry, moving the pan off and on the heat as necessary to prevent scorching, until the pork or chicken just turns opaque, 2 to 3 minutes. Add the soy sauce and pepper to taste and stir-fry for about 1 minute longer. Remove from the heat, stir in the cilantro, and set aside to cool.

Place the banana leaf pieces in a large bowl, pour in boiling water to cover, and let stand to soften, about 5 minutes; drain. Lay the leaves on a flat surface. Scoop an equal portion of the cooled rice onto the lower half of each leaf. Pat the rice to form a rectangle about 4 inches wide by 6 inches long that runs parallel with the veins of the leaf. Spoon an equal portion of the stuffing mixture down the center of each portion of rice. Roll each leaf around the rice to create a tightly wrapped cylinder, then pinch each end together and fold it back over the cylinder. Tie the packets in several places with narrow strips of softened banana leaf or cotton string, or pin each end together with a wooden toothpick or skewer. Refrigerate the rolls until well set, at least 4 hours or overnight.

To serve, return the packets to room temperature, then unwrap the rolls and, using a dampened knife blade, cut each roll into slices about ½ inch thick. Offer the Sweet Soy Sauce for dipping.

Makes 4 servings.

CRISPY RICE FLOUR CRÊPES

Chile Dipping Sauce, Vietnamese Style (page 147) or Chile Dipping Sauce, Thai Style (page 147)

BATTER
1½ cups Fresh Coconut Milk (page 140) or shaken canned coconut milk
1 cup rice flour
½ teaspoon sugar
½ teaspoon salt
1 teaspoon ground turmeric

FILLING
4 tablespoons canola oil or other high-quality vegetable oil
2 cups thinly sliced shallot
2 tablespoons minced garlic
4 cups thinly sliced flavorful fresh mushrooms such as chanterelle, portobello, porcini, or shiitake
3 cups thinly shredded cabbage, preferably napa or other Asian variety
½ cup grated fresh coconut or unsweetened dried coconut
1 cup cilantro (coriander) leaves
2 tablespoons fish sauce
Freshly ground white pepper
4 cups mung bean sprouts

Canola oil or other high-quality vegetable oil for cooking crêpes
Fresh cilantro (coriander) sprigs for garnish
Green onion "brushes" for garnish (optional)

Prepare the selected sauce as directed and set aside.

To make the batter, if using Fresh Coconut Milk, prepare as directed. In a bowl or a blender, combine all the batter ingredients and beat with a wire whisk or blend until smooth. Refrigerate until cooking time. Stir well to blend just before cooking; if the mixture becomes too thick to pour easily, thin with a little water or coconut milk to the consistency of heavy cream.

To make the filling, place a wok, large sauté pan, or large, heavy skillet over high heat. When the pan is hot, add 2 tablespoons of the oil and swirl to coat the pan. When the oil is hot, but not yet smoking, add the shallot and garlic and stir-fry until well coated with the oil, about 1 minute. Add the mushrooms and stir-fry until the mushrooms are tender, about 3 minutes. Transfer to a bowl and set aside. Return the pan to the heat and add the remaining 2 tablespoons oil. When the oil is hot but not yet smoking, add the cabbage and coconut and stir-fry until the cabbage wilts, about 2 minutes. Return the mushroom mixture to the pan. Add the cilantro, fish sauce, and pepper to taste and stir-fry until heated through, about 1 minute. Remove from the heat and stir in the bean sprouts. Set aside.

Recipe continues on page 30

BAHN XEO
...
Vietnamese

NUOM AM BAING
...
Cambodian

KANOM BUENG YUAN
...
Thai

CRISPY RICE FLOUR CRÊPES

Stir-fried shrimp and pork are traditional fillings for these crunchy crêpes, sometimes called crispy omelets, but my vegetable mixture is equally tasty. Vary the filling according to whim.

In Vietnam, the crêpes are sometimes served as roll ups, as described in the recipe for Shrimp Pops (page 78). Diners break off pieces of the filled crêpe and roll it up in lettuce leaves with fresh herbs and bits of vegetables before dipping it in the sauce and eating it out of hand. ❧

Preheat an oven to 200° F if serving all the crêpes at one time.

To cook the crêpes, in an 8-inch nonstick skillet, pour in 2 tablespoons oil and place over medium-high heat. When the oil is hot but not yet smoking, using a measuring cup, pour in ⅓ cup of the crêpe batter and quickly tilt and rotate the pan to spread the batter to form a thin pancake. Cook until brown and crispy on the bottom, 3 to 5 minutes. Using a wide spatula, lift the crêpe from the pan and drain off as much oil as possible, then transfer the crêpe to a work surface. Spoon about ¾ cup of the filling mixture over one-half of the crêpe, then fold the other half of the crêpe over the filling. Serve immediately as described below or transfer to a baking sheet and keep warm in the oven. Repeat this process to make and fill 5 more crêpes, adding oil to the skillet as needed to equal 2 tablespoons for cooking each crêpe.

To serve, divide the sauce among 6 small bowls and position a bowl at each place. Place each crêpe on a separate plate, garnish with cilantro sprigs and onion "brushes" (if using), and serve immediately.

Makes 6 servings.

FRESH SPRING OR SUMMER ROLLS

Chile Dipping Sauce, Vietnamese Style (page 147)

FILLING
About 4 cups water
54 medium-sized shrimp (about 1 pound)
3 ounces very thin, wiry dried rice noodles (vermicelli)
1 cup fresh cilantro (coriander) leaves
1 cup shredded carrot
1 cup mung bean sprouts
1 cup fresh mint leaves
9 tender lettuce leaves such as Bibb (Boston) or other soft-leaf varieties, torn lengthwise in half, washed, dried, wrapped, and chilled to crisp

18 round rice paper wrappers (Vietnamese *banh trang*), each about 8 inches in diameter
Fresh mint sprigs for garnish

Prepare the Chile Dipping Sauce as directed and set aside.

To make the filling, in a large saucepan, bring the water to a boil over high heat. Drop the shrimp into the boiling water and cook until they turn bright pink, 3 to 5 minutes. Drain and rinse in cold water to prevent further cooking. Drain again, then peel and devein. Cover and refrigerate until needed.

Prepare the rice noodles as directed on page 159 and set aside; drain well just before using. Prepare the remaining filling ingredients and refrigerate until needed.

To assemble the rolls, place the filling ingredients and the wrappers on a kitchen work surface and fill a wide, shallow bowl with warm water. Working with 1 sheet at a time, dip each rice paper round in the warm water to soften. Transfer the wrapper to a flat surface. Place 3 shrimp in a row down the center of the rice paper and a cilantro leaf on either side of the middle shrimp. Sprinkle about 1 tablespoon each of the noodles and carrot over the shrimp, then top with a few bean sprouts and mint and cilantro leaves. Cover with a piece of the lettuce. Fold the bottom of the rice paper up over the filling, then tuck in each side to encase the filling. Fold the top of the rice paper down to meet the top edge of the filling, then roll up from the bottom to form a cylinder with the ingredients showing through the top. Place seam side down on a tray or platter and cover with damp paper toweling. Soften, fill, and roll up the remaining wrappers in the same way. Serve immediately, or cover with damp paper toweling and refrigerate for up to 4 hours.

To serve, distribute the dipping sauce among 6 individual bowls. Arrange 3 of the rolls and a bowl of sauce on individual plates and garnish with mint sprigs.

Makes 6 servings.

Variations on page 32

GOI CHON
• • •
Vietnamese

MIANG YUAN
• • •
Thai

FRESH SPRING OR SUMMER ROLLS

*L*ike many popular Southeast Asian dishes, fresh (unfried) spring rolls, also called summer rolls or salad rolls, originated in China. These refreshing roll ups are filled with cooked seafood or meats, a variety of fresh vegetables and herbs, and often rice noodles. My recipe calls for softened rice papers to encase the rolls, which are known as goi chon in Vietnam, lott in Cambodia, and miang yuan in northeastern Thailand. The tissue-thin wrappers offer a glimpse of the colorful fillings.

Other parts of Southeast Asia use thin crêpelike disks made from wheat flour for wrapping their rolls, which are variously known as poh pia in

Singapore and Malaysia, kau pyan

in Myanmar (Burma), and lumpia

in the Philippines. Directions for

making these are given in the

variation following the recipe.

The filling may be varied by adding

shredded cooked chicken or pork on

top of the noodles, or by omitting the

shrimp and tossing flaked cooked

crab meat or fish, shredded cooked

chicken or meat, or crumbled tofu

with the other filling ingredients.

For large groups, arrange the

wrappers and all of the filling

ingredients on platters, trays, or in

bowls on the table and let guests

assemble their own rolls. Provide

each diner with a small bowl of

dipping sauce and a wide bowl of hot

water for softening the rice paper

wrappers. ❧

VARIATIONS

Wheat Flour-Wrapped Spring Rolls (*lumpia, kau pyan*, or *poh pia*). Purchase round fresh or frozen wheat flour wrappers, sometimes sold as egg roll skins in Asian markets; thoroughly thaw frozen wrappers in the refrigerator before using. (The egg roll wrappers commonly sold in supermarket dairy cases are too thick for making fresh rolls.) It is not necessary to soften these flour wrappers in hot water as directed for rice paper wrappers, but keep them covered with damp paper toweling to prevent the surface from drying out. Fill as directed in the recipe. Alternative dipping sauces include one of the peanut sauces (pages 150-152) or Sweet Chile-Garlic Dipping Sauce (page 146).

Fried Spring Rolls. See *James McNair's Pasta Cookbook* for complete directions for preparing these crispy nuggets.

*YUM SAPBHALOT
KWAYTIOW*
• • •
Thai

PINEAPPLE NOODLE SALAD

*T*his refreshing salad is inspired

by a traditional snack sold by Thai

street vendors. Rice noodles are

preferable for authentic flavor, but

fresh or dried thin wheat noodles

such as Japanese somen *can be*

substituted. Cooked chicken, pork,

or shrimp can be tossed with the

pineapple mixture to create a

heartier dish. ❧

¼ cup coconut cream scooped from the top of chilled Fresh Coconut Milk (page 140) or unshaken canned coconut milk
9 ounces dried rice noodles, about ⅛ inch wide

DRESSING
¼ cup freshly squeezed lime juice
2 tablespoons fish sauce
2 tablespoons sugar
1 tablespoon minced Pickled Garlic (page 155), or 1 teaspoon minced fresh garlic

2 cups well-drained fresh or canned pineapple chunks
2 tablespoons slivered fresh ginger
2 teaspoons minced fresh red or green hot chile, or to taste
2 tablespoons thinly sliced green onion, including green tops
1 tablespoon finely chopped red sweet pepper
1 tablespoon finely chopped unsalted dry-roasted cashews or peanuts
Fresh mint or cilantro (coriander) leaves for garnish

If using Fresh Coconut Milk, prepare as directed and refrigerate until chilled. If using canned coconut milk, reserve for later use.

Prepare the rice noodles as directed on page 159, drain well, and transfer to a bowl.

Scoop ¼ cup of the coconut cream from the top of the chilled fresh or canned coconut milk. Add to the noodles and toss gently to coat thoroughly. (The remaining coconut milk should be covered and refrigerated for another purpose.)

To make the dressing, in a small bowl, combine the lime juice, fish sauce, and sugar and whisk or stir to dissolve the sugar. Stir in the garlic.

In a bowl, combine the pineapple, ginger, and chile. Add the dressing and toss to coat well.

To serve, mound the noodles on a serving dish. Spoon the pineapple mixture over the top of the noodles and sprinkle with the green onion, sweet pepper, cashews or peanuts, and mint or cilantro leaves.

Makes 6 servings.

COCONUT NOODLES

2 cups Fresh Coconut Milk (page 140) or shaken canned coconut milk
9 ounces dried rice noodles, about ⅛ inch wide
5 tablespoons canola oil or other high-quality vegetable oil
1½ cups peeled, seeded, drained, and chopped ripe or canned tomato
1 tablespoon paprika
½ cup chopped shallot
8 ounces boneless tender pork, thinly sliced
⅓ cup palm sugar
2 tablespoons bottled Chinese brown or yellow bean sauce (*jiang*)
1½ tablespoons fish sauce
10 ounces mung bean sprouts
⅓ cup cubed fried tofu
3 tablespoons minced green onion, including green tops
2 tablespoons coarsely chopped unsalted dry-roasted peanuts
Lime wedges for serving
Toasted shredded coconut

If using Fresh Coconut Milk, prepare as directed and set aside. If using canned coconut milk, reserve for later use.

Prepare the noodles as described on page 159, drain well, and set aside.

Place a wok, large sauté pan, or large, heavy skillet over medium-high heat. When the pan is hot, add 3 tablespoons of the oil and swirl to coat the pan. When the oil is hot but not yet smoking, add the tomato and paprika and stir-fry until the tomato is soft and falling apart, about 5 minutes. Add the noodles and stir-fry until well coated with the tomato-oil mixture, about 2 minutes. Transfer to a bowl and set aside.

Add the remaining 2 tablespoons oil to the pan over medium-high heat. When the oil is hot, add the shallot and pork and stir-fry for about 1 minute. Stir in the coconut milk, sugar, bean sauce, and fish sauce and bring to a boil. Cook, stirring frequently, until well combined and flavorful, about 2 minutes. Reduce the heat to low, stir in the noodles, bean sprouts, and tofu, and simmer until the noodles are tender, about 2 minutes.

Transfer to a serving dish, sprinkle with the green onion and peanuts, surround with the lime wedges, and serve warm or at room temperature. Offer the toasted coconut for sprinkling over each serving.

Makes 6 servings.

MEE GA-TI
Thai

COCONUT NOODLES

*W*heat noodles cooked until tender yet still firm to the bite may be used in place of the rice noodles. Chicken or peeled and deveined shrimp may be used in place of all or part of the pork.

For a festive presentation, consider serving the noodles inside fresh coconuts. To split a coconut, position the blade of a heavy cleaver where you wish to make the cut, then strike the cleaver several times with a hammer to separate the nut into two pieces. ◗

KWAYTIOW PAHT
Thai

STIR-FRIED RICE NOODLES

There's so much flavor packed into this simple dish that meat, although traditional, is unnecessary. If you wish, however, add ½ pound boneless tender pork or beef or boned and skinned chicken, finely chopped, along with the shallot and stir-fry until opaque.

Adjust the amount of chiles according to the heat level of the available varieties. Keep in mind, however, that the finished noodles should cause your mouth to smoke.

If you have access to fresh rice noodle sheets, or make your own, cut them into noodles from ½ to 1 inch wide, a typical Thai size for stir-frying.

STIR-FRIED RICE NOODLES

9 ounces dried rice noodles, about ⅛ inch wide
¼ cup canola oil or other high-quality vegetable oil, or as needed
2 cups sliced shallot
2 tablespoons finely chopped garlic
1 tablespoon chopped fresh green or red hot chile, or to taste
2 tablespoons fish sauce
2 tablespoons soy sauce
2 tablespoons oyster sauce
2 tablespoons palm sugar
Freshly ground black pepper
1 cup fresh Asian basil leaves
1 cup fresh mint leaves
Fresh Asian basil and/or mint leaves for garnish

Prepare the noodles as directed on page 159, drain well, and set aside.

Ready all the remaining ingredients and place them next to the stove.

Place a wok, large sauté pan, or large, heavy skillet over medium-high heat. When the pan is hot, add the oil and swirl to coat the pan. When the oil is hot but not yet smoking, add the shallot and stir-fry for about 1 minute. Add the garlic and chile and stir-fry for about 30 seconds longer. Stir in the fish sauce, soy sauce, oyster sauce, sugar, and pepper to taste and stir until the mixture thickens, about 5 minutes longer.

Add the drained noodles and gently stir-fry until tender yet still firm to the bite, about 1 minute, adding a little more oil if the noodles begin to stick. Add the basil and mint leaves and gently toss the noodles until the leaves wilt, about 45 seconds. Remove from the heat.

Transfer the noodles to a serving platter or divide them among 4 to 6 individual bowls. Garnish with herb leaves and serve warm or at room temperature.

Makes 4 to 6 servings.

BEEF SOUP WITH NOODLES

STOCK
6 pounds beef bones with some meat attached, such as ribs or shanks
1 pound boneless beef chuck, in one piece
2 yellow onions, unpeeled, sliced
1 piece fresh ginger, about 3 inches long, peeled and thinly sliced
1 cinnamon stick, about 3½ inches long
5 whole star anise pods
1 teaspoon black peppercorns
Salt or fish sauce

10 ounces boneless sirloin or other tender beef, trimmed of all excess fat
    and connective tissue
9 ounces dried rice noodles, about ⅛ inch wide
10 ounces mung bean sprouts

ADDITIONS AND SEASONINGS
3 ripe tomatoes, cut in half lengthwise, then sliced
6 green onions, including green tops, thinly sliced
1 red or yellow onion, very thinly sliced, then cut into half rings
3 or 4 fresh green or red hot chiles, thinly sliced or chopped
1 cup fresh cilantro (coriander) leaves
1 cup fresh mint leaves or sprigs
1 cup fresh Asian basil leaves or sprigs
Fish sauce
Red Chile Sauce (page 148), bottled red chile sauce (Indonesian *sambal ulek* or
    Vietnamese *tuong ot*), or bottled chile-garlic sauce (Vietnamese *tuong ot toi*)
Lime or lemon wedges

To make the stock, quickly rinse the bones and chuck under cold running water. Place on a cutting surface and trim off excess fat.

In a large stockpot, combine the bones with water to cover. Place over medium heat, bring to a boil, and cook for 10 minutes. Drain. Add fresh cold water to cover by about 2 inches and return to a boil. Using a slotted utensil or wire skimmer, remove any foamy scum that rises to the surface. Continue cooking until the foaming stops, about 15 minutes.

Add the chuck, onion slices, ginger, cinnamon stick, star anise, and peppercorns to the stock and reduce the heat so that the mixture barely simmers. Cover and simmer until the chuck is tender but not falling apart, 1½ to 2 hours. Remove the chuck and set aside to cool, then cover and refrigerate until needed. Season the stock lightly with salt or fish sauce and continue to simmer the stock until it is well flavored, 6 to 8 hours longer.

Recipe continues on page 42

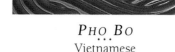

*I*n Vietnam this hearty soup is a favorite breakfast treat, but may be enjoyed at any time of the day. Both in Vietnam and in Vietnamese communities in America, entire restaurants are devoted to this singular fare.

Other traditional additions include cooked meatballs and sliced tripe.

Eight-pointed star anise pods hold tiny seeds that impart their distinct flavor to this soup; they're available in Asian markets and many supermarkets alongside other spices.

For ease in preparation, make the stock the day before serving and refrigerate overnight. ◗

When the stock is ready, remove from the heat and let cool for a few minutes. Line a colander or sieve with several layers of dampened cheesecloth and place in a large bowl set in a larger bowl filled with ice. Strain the slightly cooled stock through the colander or sieve into the bowl, pressing against the onions and meat to release all the liquid; there should be about 3 quarts. Discard the bones and their meat, onions, and spices. Season the stock to taste with salt or fish sauce and stir occasionally until cold, then cover tightly and refrigerate until well chilled, preferably overnight. When the stock is well chilled, remove any fat that has solidified on the surface.

Quickly rinse the raw beef under cold running water and pat dry with paper toweling. To facilitate slicing, wrap the beef in freezer wrap or plastic wrap and place in a freezer until very cold but not frozen hard, about 2 hours.

Transfer the stock to a stockpot or large saucepan, place over medium-high heat, and bring to a boil, then reduce the heat to maintain a simmer, cover, and keep warm while you prepare the remaining ingredients.

Prepare the noodles as directed on page 159 and let stand in cold water until serving time. Slice the cooked chuck and the chilled raw beef across the grain as thinly as possible. Place the chuck, raw beef, and bean sprouts in separate bowls alongside the simmering broth.

Prepare and arrange as many of the additions and seasonings as you wish in bowls and/or on a large platter and place on the table, or divide among individual serving trays.

To serve, drain the noodles and place alongside the simmering broth. Divide the noodles, chuck, raw beef, and bean sprouts evenly among large warmed soup bowls. Ladle the hot stock over the ingredients; it will quickly cook the raw beef slices. Serve immediately. Diners select additions and seasonings to add to their bowls to taste.

Makes 6 to 8 servings.

VARIATION
Chicken Soup with Noodles (*pho ga*). Substitute 6 pounds bony chicken pieces for the beef bones when making the stock. Poach a whole chicken in place of the chuck, removing it from the stock as soon as it is very tender. Shred the cooled chicken and add the meat to the finished stock. Omit the raw beef.

SPICY CHICKEN SOUP

1 chicken, about 3 pounds, cut up
About 2 quarts homemade chicken stock or canned reduced-sodium
    chicken broth
1 large yellow onion, quartered
3 fresh lemongrass stalks, bruised with a blunt implement
1 piece fresh galanga or ginger, about 2 inches long, peeled and coarsely
    chopped
2 cinnamon sticks, each about 3½ inches long
1 teaspoon cardamom seeds
½ teaspoon black peppercorns
Salt or fish sauce

SEASONING PASTE (INDONESIAN *BUMBU* OR MALAYSIAN *REMPAH*)
1 cup coarsely chopped shallot
1 tablespoon coarsely chopped fresh galanga or ginger
½ teaspoon firm dried shrimp paste (Indonesian *trasi* or Malaysian *blachan*),
    crumbled
2 teaspoons coriander seeds
2 teaspoons fennel seeds
1½ teaspoons cumin seeds

¼ cup canola oil or other high-quality vegetable oil
About 1 tablespoon palm sugar
About 1 teaspoon salt
4 ounces mung bean noodles

ADDITIONS AND SEASONINGS
Red Chile Sauce (page 148) or bottled red chile sauce (Indonesian *sambal
    ulek* or Vietnamese *tuong ot*)
Cooked Red Chile Sauce (page 149) or bottled cooked red chile sauce
    (Indonesian *sambal bajak*)
Sliced green onions, including green tops
Mung bean sprouts
Chopped fresh celery leaves, preferably Chinese variety (Indonesian *seledri*)
Chopped fresh red or green hot chiles
Crumbled potato chips
Diced boiled new potatoes
Chopped or sliced hard-cooked eggs or chopped egg yolk

Quickly rinse the chicken under cold running water and pat dry with paper
toweling.

In a large stockpot, combine the stock or broth, dark meat chicken pieces (reserve
the breast for later use), yellow onion, lemongrass, chopped galanga or ginger,

Recipe continues on page 44

SOTO AYAM
· · ·
Indonesian and Malaysian

SPICY CHICKEN SOUP

*This flavorful meal-in-a-bowl
originated in Java but is now served
throughout Malaysia and Indonesia.
As in the recipe for Beef Soup with
Noodles (page 41), the stock may be
cooled after straining, then covered
and refrigerated to allow for removal
of any fat that has solidified on the
surface.*

*Rice noodles, prepared as directed on
page 159, may be substituted for the
mung bean noodles.*

*Offer several of the suggested
additions and seasonings for diners to
choose among for embellishing their
servings. Slices of compressed rice
(lontong) are traditional and may
be prepared as directed on page 46
of James McNair's Rice Cookbook.*

43

Other typical offerings include Corn Fritters (page 57) and Fried Shallot (page 157). ❧

cinnamon, cardamom seeds, and peppercorns. Bring to a boil over medium-high heat, then reduce the heat to maintain a simmer, cover, and cook for 25 minutes.

Add the chicken breast to the soup and simmer, covered, until the breast just turns opaque, 15 to 20 minutes longer. Remove the chicken pieces from the stock and set aside to cool. Remove the stock from the heat and let cool for a few minutes.

Line a colander or sieve with several layers of dampened cheesecloth and place in a large bowl. Strain the stock through the colander or sieve into the bowl, pressing against the onion to release all the liquid; there should be about 2 quarts. Discard the onion and seasonings. Season with salt or fish sauce to taste. Transfer the stock to a clean stockpot and set aside.

As soon as the chicken is cool enough to handle, pull off and discard the skin and bones. Cut the meat into bite-sized pieces, cover, and refrigerate.

To make the seasoning paste, in a food processor, blender, or heavy mortar with a pestle, combine the shallot, galanga or ginger, shrimp paste, and coriander, fennel, and cumin seeds. Grind to a thick paste, adding about 1 tablespoon of water if needed to facilitate blending.

Place a wok, sauté pan, or heavy skillet over medium heat. When the pan is hot, add the oil and swirl to coat the pan. When the oil is hot, add the seasoning paste and cook, stirring constantly, until the mixture is very fragrant and darker and the oil begins to separate from the paste, about 8 minutes. Remove from the heat and drain off and discard excess oil.

Place the stock over medium-high heat, and bring to a boil, then reduce the heat to maintain a simmer. Add a little of the hot stock to the cooked paste and blend well, then stir the mixture into the stock. Stir in sugar and salt to taste, cover, and simmer while you prepare the remaining ingredients.

Place the noodles in a bowl, cover with hot water, and let stand until softened but still firm to the bite, about 10 minutes, then drain. Using kitchen scissors, cut into short lengths and set aside.

Prepare and arrange as many of the additions and seasonings as you wish in bowls and/or on a large platter and place on the table, or divide among individual serving trays.

Stir the chicken and noodles into the simmering stock and heat through, about 5 minutes.

To serve, ladle the soup into large warmed soup bowls and serve immediately. Diners select additions and seasonings to add to their bowls to taste.

Makes 6 servings.

MUSHROOM COCONUT SOUP

4 cups Fresh Coconut Milk (page 140) or shaken canned coconut milk
2 tablespoons canola oil or other high-quality vegetable oil, if using fresh
   mushrooms
12 ounces fresh meaty mushrooms such as shiitake or portobello, sliced or cut
   into pieces of equal size, or 2 cups drained canned whole straw mushrooms,
   or a combination of fresh mushrooms and canned straw mushrooms
2 cups homemade vegetable stock, or 1 cup canned vegetable broth diluted
   with 1 cup water
3 tablespoons minced fresh galanga or ginger
2 tablespoons minced fresh lemongrass, tender bulb portion only
2 teaspoons minced fresh hot chile, preferably red Thai bird variety, or to taste
1 tablespoon slivered fresh or thawed frozen kaffir lime leaves
⅛ teaspoon black or white peppercorns
3 tablespoons fish sauce
1 tablespoon freshly squeezed lime juice
1½ teaspoons palm sugar, or to taste
2 tablespoons finely chopped green onion, including green tops

If using Fresh Coconut Milk, prepare as directed and set aside. If using canned
coconut milk, reserve for later use.

If using fresh mushrooms, in a wok or skillet, heat the oil over high heat. Add the
mushrooms and stir-fry for 1 minute. Reduce the heat to medium and stir-fry until
the mushrooms are tender, 3 to 5 minutes longer. Remove from the heat and set
aside. If using canned straw mushrooms, set aside.

In a large saucepan, combine the coconut milk, vegetable stock or broth, galanga or
ginger, lemongrass, chile, lime leaves, and peppercorns. Place over medium-high
heat and bring to a boil. Reduce the heat to maintain a simmer and cook,
uncovered, for 15 minutes.

Stir the fish sauce, lime juice, sugar, and the reserved mushrooms into the
simmering soup and simmer for about 3 minutes longer. Remove from the heat,
taste, and adjust with fish sauce, sugar, and/or lime juice to achieve a balance of
salty, sweet, and sour.

To serve, ladle the hot soup into warmed bowls, sprinkle evenly with the green
onion, and serve immediately.

Makes 6 servings.

VARIATION
Chicken-Coconut Soup (tom kha gai). Reduce the amount of mushrooms to 1 cup
and substitute homemade chicken stock or canned broth for the vegetable stock or
broth. Slice 2 boned and skinned chicken breast halves into bite-sized pieces and
add to the simmering soup. Cook just until the chicken turns opaque; do not allow
to boil or the chicken will be overcooked and tough.

TOM YAM HED GA-TI
Thai

MUSHROOM COCONUT SOUP

My favorite Southeast Asian soup
is Thai tom kha gai, a fragrant
blend of chicken, coconut milk,
galanga, lemongrass, and other
seasonings. For my vegetarian
friends, however, I created this
soup, which captures much of the
essence of the Thai original. The
variation can be used by those who
wish to try the traditional version.

Straw mushrooms (volvaria
esculenta), imported canned or
dried from China and Southeast
Asia, have very rounded, elongated
heads and delicate flavor. ❧

47

LEAF ROLLS WITH TREASURES

1 head butter lettuce or other tender leaf variety, or 1 bunch tender young
   spinach, separated into individual leaves, then washed, dried, wrapped, and
   chilled to crisp

COCONUT SPREAD
¼ cup fish sauce
¼ cup palm sugar
¼ cup minced or ground unsalted dry-roasted peanuts
¼ cup grated or minced fresh or unsweetened dried (desiccated) coconut

TOPPINGS
¼ cup shredded fresh or unsweetened dried coconut, lightly toasted
¼ cup unsalted dry-roasted peanuts
¼ cup dried tiny shrimp
¼ cup minced fresh red or green hot chile
¼ cup Pickled Ginger (page 154) or minced fresh ginger
¼ cup minced shallot
1 lime, halved, seeded, sliced about ⅛ inch thick, and cut into tiny pieces

Prepare the lettuce or spinach leaves and refrigerate until serving time.

To make the Coconut Spread, in a small saucepan, combine the fish sauce, sugar,
peanuts, and coconut. Place over medium heat and bring to a boil, then cook,
stirring frequently, until the mixture is fairly thick and syrupy, 2 to 3 minutes.
Remove from the heat and set aside to cool to room temperature. (The spread
will thicken further as it cools. If it becomes too thick, thin with a little warm
water to a spreadable consistency.)

To serve, transfer the spread to a small dish. Place each of the toppings in a separate
small dish. Place the lettuce or spinach on a serving dish or tray and arrange the
small dishes of spread and toppings alongside.

To eat, each diner smears a little of the spread onto a lettuce or spinach leaf,
sprinkles on toppings to taste, and then folds the leaf around the toppings.

Makes 4 servings.

MIENG KUM
Thai

LEAF ROLLS WITH TREASURES

*O*ne rare sweltering day in San
Francisco, I enjoyed this unusual
dish for lunch at Swatdee, my former
neighborhood Thai restaurant. I was
instantly transported to tropical Asia.
The dish, which makes a wonderful
Western-style appetizer, is frequently
served on festive occasions in
Thailand, where a variety of edible
tree leaves are used as wrappers
instead of the less-exotic lettuce and
spinach.

Rose petals or edible blossoms such as
borage, nasturtium, or viola make a
festive addition to the topping choices.
Just be sure that they are nontoxic
and pesticide free. ❧

GOI DU DU
•••
Vietnamese
SOM TUM
•••
Thai
THINNBAWTHEE THOKE
•••
Burmese

GREEN PAPAYA SALAD

Throughout tropical Asia, unripe papaya is eaten as a vegetable and one of the most popular uses is in salad. In America, green papayas are often available in Asian and Spanish markets.

For a heartier dish, toss about 1 cup cooked small shrimp or shredded cooked chicken, beef, or pork into the mixture along with the tomato and other final ingredients. ❧

GREEN PAPAYA SALAD

DRESSING
¼ cup freshly squeezed lime juice
3 tablespoons fish sauce
2 teaspoons palm sugar
1 tablespoon minced or pressed garlic
2 tablespoons minced fresh red or green hot chile

3 cups peeled, seeded, and shredded green (unripe) papaya
½ cup peeled and shredded carrot
½ cup thinly slivered red sweet pepper
¼ cup coarsely chopped fresh mint
¼ cup coarsely chopped fresh cilantro (coriander)
3 tablespoons minced green onion, including green tops
½ cup peeled, seeded, drained, and chopped ripe tomato
1 tablespoon dried shrimp powder or finely ground dried shrimp (ground in a spice grinder, blender, or heavy mortar with a pestle)
2 tablespoons coarsely chopped unsalted dry-roasted peanuts
2 tablespoons sesame seeds, lightly toasted
Fresh mint sprigs for garnish

To make the dressing, in a large bowl, combine the lime juice, fish sauce, and sugar and stir to dissolve the sugar. Stir in the garlic and chile until well mixed.

Add the papaya, carrot, sweet pepper, mint, cilantro, and green onion to the dressing. Using your hands, gently squeeze the mixture to release the flavors and soften the vegetables. Add the tomato, shrimp powder or ground shrimp, peanuts, and sesame seeds and toss to mix well.

To serve, mound the salad on a serving plate or in a bowl and garnish with mint sprigs.

Makes 4 servings.

Rujak
Indonesian

SPICE ISLANDS SALAD

A dressing of sour tamarind, sweet palm sugar, devilishly hot chile sauce, and pungent shrimp paste adds a kick to fruit salad.

Any combination of fresh tropical fruits would be acceptable in place of those I've used here, but cucumber and pineapple should be included for authentic flavor. Our jicama is familiar to Southeast Asians as yam bean. Pomelo is a thick-skinned, firmer-fleshed tropical relative of grapefruit. Starfruit, or carambola, is a tropical fruit that forms perfect stars when sliced and has a mild citrus flavor. ❧

52

SPICE ISLANDS SALAD

DRESSING
1 teaspoon Cooked Red Chile Sauce (page 149) or bottled cooked red chile sauce (Indonesian *sambal bajak*), or to taste
¼ cup Tamarind Liquid (page 156)
1 slice firm dried shrimp paste (Indonesian *trasi* or Malaysian *blachan*), about ¼ inch thick and ¾ inch square
¼ cup palm sugar
½ cup water
¼ teaspoon salt

1 small cucumber, peeled, halved lengthwise, seeded, and sliced crosswise, or ½ seedless cucumber (English or hothouse), peeled in a striped pattern and sliced crosswise
1 green or ripe mango, cubed or sliced
1 cup bite-sized fresh or well-drained canned pineapple chunks
1 cup bite-sized jicama cubes or slices
1 cup bite-sized unpeeled tart green apple slices
1 pomelo or grapefruit, zest, white pith, and outer membrane cut away, then sliced between connecting membrane into segments
1 starfruit, sliced
2 tablespoons finely chopped unsalted dry-roasted peanuts (optional)

To make the dressing, if using the Cooked Red Chile Sauce, prepare as directed and set aside. If using bottled chile sauce, reserve for later use.

Prepare the Tamarind Liquid as directed and set aside.

Wrap the shrimp paste in aluminum foil. Using metal tongs, hold the paste over a flame, or place the packet in a small, dry skillet over medium-high heat or under a preheated broiler until toasted and fragrant, about 2 minutes on each side.

Unwrap the paste and place in a saucepan with the chile sauce, Tamarind Liquid, sugar, water, and salt. Place over medium heat and bring to a boil, then adjust the heat to maintain a simmer. Cook, stirring frequently, until the sugar is dissolved and the flavors are well blended, about 5 minutes. Remove from the heat and set aside to cool.

In a bowl, combine the cucumber, mango, pineapple, jicama, apple, pomelo or grapefruit, and starfruit. Add the reserved dressing and toss to mix well.

To serve, transfer the salad to a serving dish or divide among individual serving dishes and sprinkle with the chopped peanuts (if using).

Makes 6 to 8 servings.

ACAR CAMPUR
...
Indonesian

ACAR KUNING
...
Malaysian

PICKLED VEGETABLES

This vegetable combination should be altered according to seasonal availability. Offer either Red Chile Sauce (page 148) or Cooked Red Chile Sauce (page 149) or purchase bottled versions of these sambals for diners to adjust the level of heat to preference. I also enjoy a garnish of Coconut-Peanut Sprinkle (page 157) strewn over the vegetables. ❧

54

PICKLED VEGETABLES

1½ cups cauliflower florets (from about ½ small head)
1½ cups peeled baby carrots or ½-inch lengths of larger carrot
1½ cups sugar snap peas or green beans (about 6 ounces)
3 fresh small red hot chiles, stemmed and thinly sliced lengthwise, or to taste
1 tablespoon minced fresh ginger
2 teaspoons chopped garlic
2 teaspoons minced lemongrass, tender bulb portion only
1 teaspoon ground turmeric
¼ cup distilled white vinegar
1 tablespoon palm sugar
¾ cup water
2 tablespoons canola oil or other high-quality vegetable oil
1½ cups thinly sliced shallot
Salt

Place the prepared cauliflower, carrots, peas or beans, and chiles alongside the stove.

In a mini food processor, spice grinder, or heavy mortar with a pestle, blend the ginger, garlic, lemongrass, and turmeric to make a paste, adding up to 3 tablespoons water if needed to facilitate blending. Transfer to a small bowl and place next to the stove. In a small bowl, combine the vinegar, sugar, and water and place alongside the stove as well.

Place a wok, large sauté pan, or large, heavy skillet over high heat. When the pan is hot, add the oil and swirl to coat the pan. When the oil is hot but not yet smoking, add the shallot and stir-fry until soft and lightly golden, about 3 minutes. Add the ginger-garlic paste and stir-fry to coat the shallot, about 1 minute. Add the reserved vinegar mixture, cauliflower, and carrots and stir-fry, moving the pan off and on the heat as necessary to prevent scorching, about 5 minutes. Add the peas or beans, chiles, and salt to taste and stir-fry until the vegetables are crisp-tender and the sauce is slightly thickened, about 5 minutes longer.

Transfer the vegetables to a serving bowl and serve warm or at room temperature while the vegetables are still crisp.

Makes 6 servings.

CORN FRITTERS

Sweet Soy Sauce (page 149) or bottled Indonesian sweet soy sauce (*kecap manis*)
1 teaspoon Red Chile Sauce (page 148) or bottled red chile sauce
   (Indonesian *sambal ulek* or Vietnamese *tuong ot*)
2 cups fresh, thawed frozen, or drained canned corn kernels
2 teaspoons minced or pressed garlic
1½ teaspoons minced fresh lemongrass, tender bulb portion only
1 teaspoon fish sauce, or to taste
1 egg, lightly beaten
3 tablespoons rice flour
2 tablespoons all-purpose flour
½ teaspoon baking powder
1 tablespoon ground coriander
½ teaspoon ground cumin
½ teaspoon ground ginger
¼ teaspoon freshly ground black pepper, or to taste
Canola oil or other high-quality vegetable oil for deep-frying

If using Sweet Soy Sauce and/or Red Chile Sauce, prepare as directed and set each aside. If using bottled sauces, reserve for later use.

In a bowl, combine the corn, chile sauce, garlic, lemongrass, fish sauce, and egg and mix well. Add the flours, baking powder, and ground coriander, cumin, ginger, and pepper. Stir to form a thick batter.

In a wok, deep-fat fryer, or large, deep pan such as a dutch oven, pour in oil to a depth of 2 inches. Heat to 350° F, or until a small piece of bread dropped into the hot oil turns golden brown within about 45 seconds. Preheat an oven to 200° F. Place a wire rack over a baking sheet; set aside.

Using wet hands, gently press a heaping tablespoon of the corn batter between your palms to form a roughly shaped patty. Transfer to a slotted utensil and carefully lower into the hot oil. Form a few other patties and add to the oil; avoid crowding the pan. Cook until the bottoms of the fritters are crisp and golden brown, about 2 minutes, then turn and cook until the other sides are golden brown, about 1 minute longer. Using a slotted utensil, remove the fritters to the wire rack to drain well, then place in the preheated oven to keep warm. Cook the remaining corn batter in the same manner, allowing the oil to return to 350° F between each batch.

Serve warm with the sweet soy sauce.

Makes 4 to 6 servings.

VARIATION
Thai Corn Fritters (*tod man khao pohd*). Substitute 1 tablespoon Red Curry Paste (page 142) or Yellow Curry Paste (page 144) or canned Thai red or yellow curry paste for the chile sauce. Omit the ground coriander, cumin, and ginger. Serve with Sweet Chile-Garlic Dipping Sauce (page 146).

PERKEDEL GORENG
• • •
Indonesian

CORN FRITTERS

*F*resh corn is often added to Southeast Asian coconut milk drinks and puddings or used to make these puffy crisp fritters. My recipe is Indonesian-style, yet can easily be turned into a Thai dish, as suggested in the variation that follows.

You may wish to offer additional chile sauce at the table. ❧

KHAYANTHEE PAUNG
· · ·
Burmese

STEAMED EGGPLANT

*G*entle steaming ensures the characteristically creamy texture of this dish. Choose slender lavender (Chinese) or dark purple (Japanese) eggplants. ❧

58

1 teaspoon Red Chile Sauce (page 148) or bottled red chile sauce (Indonesian *sambal ulek* or Vietnamese *tuong ot*), or 2 teaspoons minced fresh red hot chile
4 slender Asian eggplants (see recipe introduction)
2 tablespoons canola oil or other high-quality vegetable oil
1 cup finely chopped shallot
1 tablespoon minced or pressed garlic
½ cup dried shrimp powder or finely ground dried shrimp (ground in a spice grinder, blender, or heavy mortar with a pestle)
1 tablespoon ground paprika
2 cups water
3 tablespoons soy sauce
2 tablespoons fish sauce
3 tablespoons Asian sesame oil
Fresh cilantro (coriander) leaves for garnish

If using Red Chile Sauce, prepare as directed and set aside. If using bottled chile sauce or fresh chile, reserve for later use.

To prepare for steaming, position a rack in a wok or pan that will be large enough to hold the eggplants and can be completely covered by a lid. Pour in water to a level just below the steaming rack, place over high heat, and bring to a boil, then lower the heat to achieve a simmer.

Place the eggplants on the steamer rack. Cover and steam until the eggplants are very tender when pierced with a skewer or knife but still hold their shape, 15 to 20 minutes. Adjust the heat to maintain simmering water and continuous steam throughout cooking, adding boiling water if needed to maintain water level.

Meanwhile, place a wok, large sauté pan, or large, heavy skillet over medium-high heat. When the pan is hot, add the oil and swirl to coat the pan. When the oil is hot, add the shallot and stir-fry until lightly browned, about 3 minutes. Stir in the garlic, chile sauce or chile, shrimp powder or ground shrimp, and paprika and stir-fry for about 1 minute longer. Add the water, soy sauce, fish sauce, and sesame oil and bring to a boil. Cook, stirring frequently, until the sauce is reduced to about 1 cup, about 20 minutes.

When the eggplants are done, remove to a work surface. As soon as they are cool enough to handle, carefully remove and discard the peel. Arrange the eggplants on a serving dish, spoon the sauce over them, and garnish with cilantro leaves. Serve warm or at room temperature.

Makes 4 servings.

SAMBAL GORENG
•••
Indonesian and Malaysian

FIERY FRIED GREEN VEGETABLES

*I*t was love at first bite when I
encountered a plate of crisp green
beans in a thick "dry" chile sauce at
Singapore Malaysia Restaurant in
San Francisco.

*Use any green beans (including
the Asian long beans), asparagus,
zucchini, or okra. Snap off ends and
discard any strings from green beans.
If beans are young and tender, leave
whole; cut larger beans into 1½-inch
lengths. Snap off and discard tough
ends from asparagus and use tender
spears whole; cut larger spears as for
green beans. Leave baby zucchini
whole; slice mature ones crosswise
about ¼ inch thick. Cut off and
discard stems from okra, leaving
young tender pods intact; slice larger
pods on the diagonal into 1-inch-wide
pieces. ❧*

FIERY FRIED
GREEN VEGETABLES

1 pound green vegetables (see recipe introduction for selections and
   preparations)

SEASONING PASTE (INDONESIAN *BUMBU* OR MALAYSIAN *REMPAH*)
1 tablespoon Red Chile Sauce (page 148) or bottled red chile sauce
   (Indonesian *sambal ulek* or Vietnamese *tuong ot*), or 2 tablespoons
   coarsely chopped fresh red hot chile
2 tablespoons dried shrimp
1½ cups chopped shallot
1 tablespoon coarsely chopped garlic

6 tablespoons canola oil or other high-quality vegetable oil
½ cup water
2 tablespoons tomato catsup
About 2 teaspoons palm sugar
Salt

Prepare the vegetables as directed and set aside.

To make the seasoning paste, if using Red Chile Sauce, prepare as directed and
set aside. If using bottled chile sauce or chile, reserve for later use. Place the dried
shrimp in a small bowl, add warm water to cover, and set aside to soften for about
15 minutes.

Drain the shrimp and place them in a food processor, blender, or heavy mortar with
a pestle. Add the chile sauce or chile, shallot, and garlic and blend to a thick paste,
adding up to 2 tablespoons water if needed to facilitate blending. Set aside.

Place a wok, large sauté pan, or large, heavy skillet over medium heat. When the
pan is hot, add the oil and swirl to coat the pan. When the oil is hot, add the
seasoning paste and cook, stirring constantly, until the mixture is very fragrant and
darker and the oil begins to separate from the paste, about 8 minutes. Increase the
heat to medium-high, add the prepared green vegetables, and stir-fry to coat well,
about 1 minute.

Stir the water, catsup, and sugar and salt to taste into the vegetables. Reduce the
heat to medium, cover, and cook, stirring frequently, until the vegetables are crisp-
tender, 10 to 20 minutes depending upon the size and age of the vegetables.
Transfer to a serving dish and serve warm or at room temperature.

Makes 6 servings.

GHIN THOKE
. . .
Burmese

GINGER SALAD

I use a combination of fresh and sweet pickled ginger in this "salad" from Myanmar, where it is traditionally eaten as a dessert or snack. Most Westerners, however, will prefer to eat it as an appetizer or accompaniment.

If you wish, use 1 cup of dried yellow split peas or fava beans instead of the combination given. Packaged fried fava beans and yellow split peas, sold in Japanese or Indian markets, can be used in place of the home-fried ones in the recipe. Optional additions include about ¼ cup toasted shredded coconut and/or toasted sesame seeds, and about the same amount of Fried Shallot (page 157).

½ cup dried yellow split peas
½ cup dried fava beans
Canola oil or other high-quality vegetable oil for deep-frying
½ cup unsalted dry-roasted peanuts
2 tablespoons freshly squeezed lime juice
1 tablespoon juice from Pickled Ginger (page 154) or commercial pickled ginger
2 teaspoons fish sauce, or to taste
4 teaspoons minced Pickled Garlic (page 155) or 2 teaspoons minced fresh garlic
Salt
1½ cups finely shredded green cabbage
½ cup finely shredded purple cabbage
¼ cup minced Pickled Ginger (page 154) or commercial pickled ginger
¼ cup minced fresh ginger
¼ cup minced shallot
¼ cup minced red sweet pepper mixed with 2 teaspoons minced fresh red or green hot chile, or to taste
Lime wedges for serving

Place the split peas in a saucepan and the fava beans in a second pan. Add enough water to each pan to cover the legumes by about 1 inch. Place over medium heat and bring to a boil, then reduce the heat to maintain a simmer. Cook the split peas until barely tender, 10 to 15 minutes, then drain and set aside. Cook the fava beans until the skins soften enough to be peeled off, about 20 minutes. Using a slotted utensil, remove the beans and reserve the water in the pan. Using your thumbnail, peel off and discard the skins. Return the peeled beans to the water, adjust the heat to maintain a simmer, and cook, uncovered, until the beans are plumped and barely tender, 15 to 20 minutes longer, then drain and set aside.

In a wok or heavy sauté pan, pour in oil to a depth of about 1 inch and heat to 350° F, or until a small piece of bread dropped into the hot oil turns golden brown within about 45 seconds. Carefully add the split peas to the hot oil and fry until golden brown and crisp, 3 to 4 minutes. Using a slotted utensil, transfer to paper toweling to drain well. Return the oil to 350° F, add the fava beans and fry until golden brown and crisp, 4 to 5 minutes. Drain on paper toweling. Fry and drain the peanuts in the same way; they should cook in 2 to 3 minutes. Set aside.

In a bowl, combine the lime juice, ginger juice, fish sauce, garlic, and salt to taste; mix well. Set aside.

A few minutes before serving, combine the green and purple cabbages and mound in the center of a serving plate. Arrange the fried peas and beans and peanuts, pickled and fresh ginger, shallot, and sweet pepper and chile in separate mounds around the cabbage. Pour the lime dressing over the top.

Recipe continues on page 64

A similar salad is made from steamed fresh tea leaves (laphet) that are packed in clay vessels and stored in the ground near a running stream to ensure a constant temperature. Unfortunately, this product is not imported to North America at this time, although Burmese restaurateurs seem to be able to acquire the leaves. After several unsuccessful attempts to use reconstituted dried green tea leaves, I decided not to include the recipe. If you can find laphet, prepare the salad as for ginger salad, substituting the tea leaves for the cabbage. ❧

At the table, toss the ingredients together to combine well before serving. Offer lime wedges for squeezing over individual portions.

Alternatively, in a large bowl, combine the lime juice, ginger juice, fish sauce, garlic, and salt to taste. Add the cabbages, fried peas and beans and peanuts, pickled and fresh ginger, shallot, and sweet pepper and chile and toss thoroughly. Mound on a serving plate or transfer to a serving bowl. Serve immediately, or cover and let stand for up to 1 hour before serving. Offer lime wedges for squeezing over individual portions.

Makes 8 servings.

STUFFED EGGPLANT

Tamarind Dipping Sauce (page 146)
2 teaspoons Red Chile Sauce (page 148) or bottled red chile sauce
    (Indonesian *sambal ulek* or Vietnamese *tuong ot*), or 2 tablespoons
    minced fresh red hot chile
About ¼ cup Fried Shallot (page 157)
6 small eggplants (see recipe introduction)
12 ounces boned and skinned chicken breast and/or thigh
2 tablespoons canola oil or other high-quality vegetable oil
2 tablespoons minced shallot
2 tablespoons minced garlic
½ pound peeled and cooked tiny bay shrimp
3 tablespoons fish sauce
1 teaspoon soy sauce
2 tablespoons palm sugar, or to taste
¼ cup minced fresh Asian basil, cilantro (coriander), or mint leaves
Fresh Asian basil, cilantro (coriander), or mint sprigs or whole garlic
    chives for garnish

Prepare the Tamarind Dipping Sauce as directed and set aside.

If using Red Chile Sauce, prepare as directed and set aside. If using bottled
chile sauce or fresh chile, reserve for later use.

Prepare the Fried Shallot as directed and set aside.

Steam the eggplants as described in the recipe for Steamed Eggplant on page
58. Remove the eggplants to a work surface to cool. As soon as they are cool
enough to handle, peel off and discard the skin. Cut a slit into each eggplant
on one side to create a deep pocket without cutting all the way through. Set
aside.

Quickly rinse the chicken under cold running water, then pat dry with paper
toweling. Using a very sharp cleaver or knife, chop into tiny pieces.

Place a wok, large sauté pan, or large, heavy skillet over high heat. When the
pan is hot, add the oil and swirl to coat the pan. When the oil is hot but not
yet smoking, add the shallot and stir-fry for about 1 minute. Add the garlic and
chile sauce or chile and stir-fry for about 30 seconds. Add the chicken and stir-
fry, moving the pan off and on the heat as necessary to prevent scorching, until
the meat is opaque, about 3 minutes. Add the bay shrimp, fish sauce, and soy
sauce and stir to blend well. Add the sugar and stir-fry until the sugar melts,
about 30 seconds. Add the minced basil, cilantro, or mint and stir-fry about

Recipe continues on page 66

PEEG MA KUA YAOW
Thai

STUFFED EGGPLANT

*T*his dish is inspired by a similar
preparation I sampled at Royal Thai
Restaurant in San Rafael, California.
Look for small globular eggplants or
for the slender lavender (Chinese) or
dark purple (Japanese) varieties.

In lieu of steaming, the eggplants
may be grilled until the skin is
charred and the pulp tests soft when
pierced with a wooden skewer. ◣

65

30 seconds longer. Remove from the heat and transfer the mixture to a bowl; cover to keep warm.

To serve, spoon the chicken-shrimp mixture into the pockets of the eggplants, mounding any extra mixture on top. If desired, reheat in a microwave oven. Arrange on a serving dish and spoon the tamarind sauce over the top of the stuffing and onto the dish. Sprinkle the Fried Shallot over the top and garnish with the herb sprigs or garlic chives.

Makes 6 servings.

SHRIMP OR PRAWN CHIPS

Manufactured from shrimp and tapioca flour, these featherlight wafers come in various shapes and sizes, and are sometimes tinted in a variety of colors. My choice is the large variety from Indonesia sold as prawn chips. All must be fried before eating. During cooking they more than double in size and, when the oil is at the proper temperature, turn light and crispy. If the oil is overheated, the chips brown too soon; if the oil is not hot enough, the chips will be as tough as Styrofoam.

Canola oil or other high-quality vegetable oil for deep-frying
8 ounces dried shrimp or prawn chips

In a wok, deep-fat fryer, or large, deep pan such as a dutch oven, pour in oil to a depth of 2 inches. Heat to 365° F, or until a small piece of shrimp chip dropped into the hot oil puffs up within about 3 seconds. Place a wire rack over a baking sheet; set aside.

Carefully add the chips to the hot oil, one at a time if using large ones or a few at a time if using smaller ones; avoid crowding the pan. Cook until puffed and lightly browned, about 15 seconds. Using a slotted utensil or tongs, transfer to the wire rack to drain well. Cook the remaining chips in the same manner, allowing the oil to return to 365° F between batches.

Let cool completely and serve at room temperature, or store in an airtight container for up to 3 days.

Makes 6 servings.

NOTE: If all of the chips are not fried soon after opening a package, seal the remainder in plastic bags. Should they become soft during storage, spread them on a baking sheet and place in a 250° F oven until hard and dry before attempting to fry them.

KRUPUK UDANG
...
Indonesian and Malaysian
BANH PHONG TOM
...
Vietnamese

SHRIMP OR PRAWN CHIPS

These crunchy chips make a great appetizer with any of the peanut sauces (pages 150-152) or one of the other dipping sauces on pages 146-148. They are also perfect accompaniments to curries.

Emping, a delectable wafer from Indonesia (shown on the right in the photo), is made from the seed kernels of the Genetum gnemon, a tropical tree known commonly as melinjo. Fry as directed for shrimp chips, then sprinkle lightly with salt and serve with drinks or as an accompaniment. ❧

YUM GOONG YAHNG PHET
Thai

FIERY GRILLED SHRIMP SALAD

*C*ool, crisp greens and refreshing
mint balance the fiery dressing for the
shrimp. I've also enjoyed this salad
made with home-smoked shrimp; just
follow the manufacturer's directions
for your smoker. When you don't
wish to fire up a grill or a smoker,
the shrimp can be boiled or they can
be stir-fried in a wok with a little
vegetable oil.

Avoid using bitter or assertive greens
such as curly endive (chicory) or
radicchio.

FIERY GRILLED SHRIMP SALAD

1 tablespoon Red Curry Paste (page 142) or canned Thai red curry paste
2 cups mixed young salad greens or tender lettuce leaves, washed, dried, wrapped, and chilled to crisp
1 pound medium-sized or large shrimp
Vegetable oil for brushing grill rack
1 teaspoon minced fresh lemongrass, tender bulb portion only
¼ cup chopped fresh cilantro (coriander)
6 tablespoons freshly squeezed lime juice
¼ cup fish sauce
2 tablespoons sugar
½ cup thinly sliced shallot
2 tablespoons thinly sliced green onion, including green tops
2 ounces snow peas, trimmed, parboiled until crisp-tender, then cooled in ice water and drained
½ cup fresh whole small mint leaves or chopped larger leaves
3 tablespoons fresh Asian basil leaves
Lime slices for garnish
Fresh Asian basil and/or mint sprigs for garnish
Pesticide-free nontoxic flowers such as borage, garlic, or pineapple sage for garnish (optional)

If using Red Curry Paste, prepare as directed and set aside. If using canned curry paste, reserve for later use.

Prepare the salad greens and refrigerate until serving time.

Prepare an open grill for hot direct-heat cooking.

Quickly rinse the shrimp under cold running water and pat dry with paper toweling. Set aside.

When the fire is ready, brush the grill rack or a wire mesh rack with vegetable oil. Place the shrimp on the rack and cook, turning once, until the shrimp shells turn bright pink and the meat is just opaque, 4 to 5 minutes in all. Remove from the grill to a plate to cool.

In a bowl, combine the lemongrass, cilantro, lime juice, fish sauce, sugar, and curry paste. Blend well.

When the shrimp are cool enough to handle, peel and devein. Add them to the fish sauce mixture, along with the shallot, green onion, and snow peas; toss well.

Line a serving plate with the chilled greens and sprinkle with the mint leaves and basil leaves. Using a slotted utensil, remove the shrimp and snow peas from the dressing and arrange on the greens. Drizzle the dressing over the greens. Garnish with the lime slices, herb sprigs, and flowers (if using) and serve immediately.

Makes 4 servings.

GAENG SAPBHALOT GOONG
...
Thai

PINEAPPLE SHRIMP CURRY

*U*sing canned pineapple makes this curry quick and easy to prepare, although you may wish to substitute fresh fruit; you'll need 1 cup chopped fruit and 2 cups cut into bite-sized pieces. When using fresh pineapple, you may wish to create an attractive presentation by cutting off the top third of the fruit or by cutting the fruit in half horizontally and slicing out the flesh; use the pineapple shell as a serving container. ☙

PINEAPPLE SHRIMP CURRY

2 cups Fresh Coconut Milk (page 140) or unshaken canned coconut milk
2 tablespoons Yellow Curry Paste (page 144) or canned Thai yellow curry paste, or to taste
1 pound large shrimp
1 can (8 ounces) crushed pineapple, drained
3 tablespoons fish sauce
1 tablespoon palm sugar
1 can (15¾ ounces) pineapple chunks, drained
2 tablespoons freshly squeezed lime juice
3 tablespoons thinly sliced green onion, including green tops
3 tablespoons shredded fresh mint leaves
Shredded or minced zest of 1 lime
Whole fresh mint leaves for garnish

If using Fresh Coconut Milk, prepare as directed and refrigerate until chilled. If using canned coconut milk, reserve for later use.

If using Yellow Curry Paste, prepare as directed and set aside. If using canned curry paste, reserve for later use.

Peel and devein the shrimp, quickly rinse under cold running water, pat dry with paper toweling, and slice in half lengthwise. Cover and refrigerate until needed.

Scoop ½ cup of the coconut cream from the top of the chilled fresh or canned coconut milk and transfer to a wok or heavy saucepan. Place over medium heat and bring to a boil. Stir in the curry paste and cook, stirring constantly, until very fragrant, about 5 minutes.

Stir the remaining 1½ cups coconut milk to achieve a smooth consistency, then slowly stir it into the curry paste mixture. Add the crushed pineapple, fish sauce, and sugar. Bring to a simmer and cook for about 3 minutes.

Add the shrimp to the simmering curry and cook until the shrimp curl and turn opaque, 1 to 2 minutes. Stir in the pineapple chunks, lime juice, and about 2 tablespoons *each* of the green onion and shredded mint and heat through.

Ladle into a serving bowl and sprinkle with the lime zest and the remaining green onion and shredded mint. Garnish with whole mint leaves and serve warm.

Makes 4 servings.

SAMBUL UDANG
...
Indonesian and Malaysian

SHRIMP IN CHILE SAUCE

To re-create a typical Malaysian breakfast, serve these spicy shrimp with Crispy Anchovies and Peanuts (page 158), Malaysian-Style Coconut Rice (page 18), cucumber slices, and chopped or sliced hard-cooked egg. The dish is also great with plain rice for any meal. ❧

74

SEASONING PASTE (INDONESIAN *BUMBU* OR MALAYSIAN *REMPAH*)
1½ tablespoons Red Chile Sauce (page 148) or bottled red chile sauce (Indonesian *sambal ulek* or Vietnamese *tuong ot*)
1 cup coarsely chopped shallot
1 tablespoon coarsely chopped garlic
1 tablespoon sliced fresh lemongrass, tender bulb portion only
1 tablespoon coarsely chopped fresh galanga or ginger
1 tablespoon coarsely chopped candlenuts
1 slice firm dried shrimp paste (Indonesian *trasi* or Malaysian *blachan*), about ¼ inch thick and ¾ inch square, crumbled

1 pound large shrimp
6 tablespoons canola oil or other high-quality vegetable oil
1½ cups sliced shallot
1 large ripe tomato, peeled, cored, and cut into wedges
About 2 tablespoons palm sugar
About 1 teaspoon salt
About 2 tablespoons freshly squeezed lime juice
Fresh cilantro (coriander) leaves for garnish

To make the seasoning paste, if using Red Chile Sauce, prepare as directed and set aside. If using bottled chile sauce, reserve for later use.

In a food processor, blender, or heavy mortar with a pestle, combine the chopped shallot, garlic, lemongrass, galanga or ginger, nuts, shrimp paste, and chile sauce and blend to a thick paste, adding about 1 tablespoon of water if needed to facilitate blending. Set aside.

Peel and devein the shrimp, quickly rinse under cold running water, and pat dry with paper toweling. Set aside.

Place a wok, large sauté pan, or large, heavy skillet over medium heat. When the pan is hot, add the oil and swirl to coat the pan. When the oil is hot, add the seasoning paste and cook, stirring constantly, until the mixture is very fragrant and darker and the oil begins to separate from the paste, about 8 minutes.

Add the sliced shallot and stir-fry for about 1 minute. Add the shrimp and tomato and stir-fry until the shrimp turn opaque, 6 to 8 minutes longer. Season to taste with sugar, salt, and lime juice. Transfer to a serving bowl, garnish with cilantro leaves, and serve warm.

Makes 6 servings.

GRILLED SQUID

MARINADE
¼ cup fish sauce
2 tablespoons soy sauce
2 tablespoons minced or pressed garlic
1 teaspoon freshly ground white pepper
1 teaspoon sugar

12 small whole squid

CILANTRO SAUCE
6 tablespoons minced fresh cilantro, including some roots and lower
  stem portions
1 tablespoon minced or pressed garlic
¼ cup freshly squeezed lime juice
¼ cup fish sauce
2 tablespoons sugar, or to taste
1 teaspoon freshly ground white pepper, or to taste

Vegetable oil for brushing grill rack
Tender lettuce leaves for garnish
Chile "flowers" for garnish (optional)

To make the marinade, in a bowl, combine all the ingredients, mix well, and set aside.

Clean the squid as described in the recipe introduction, place them in the marinade, cover, and refrigerate for at least 2 hours or, preferably, overnight.

About 30 minutes before cooking, place 12 bamboo skewers in a shallow container, cover with water, and set aside to soak. Prepare an open grill for hot direct-heat cooking.

To make the Cilantro Sauce, in a bowl, combine all the ingredients and mix well. Set aside to use as a dipping sauce.

Remove the squid from the marinade and thread 1 sac and 1 set of tentacles onto each skewer.

When the fire is ready, lightly brush the grill rack with oil. Place the skewered squid on the rack and grill for about 1 minute. Turn and grill the second side until the squid is just opaque, about 1 minute longer.

To serve, arrange the skewered squid on a serving dish and place the dipping sauce alongside. Garnish with lettuce leaves and chile "flowers" (if using).

Makes 4 servings.

PLA MUK YANG
•••
Thai

GRILLED SQUID

*S*callops or shrimp may be
substituted for the squid in this
preparation that makes a terrific
Western-style appetizer.

To clean the squid, hold under cold
running water and pull off the
speckled membrane that covers the
sac, or hood, then gently pull to
separate the sac from the tentacles.
Pull out and discard the shell, or
sword, and any remaining contents
from inside the sac. Rinse the inside
of the sac, pat dry, and set aside.
Slice off the tentacles portion just
above the eyes and discard everything
except the tentacles. Squeeze out and
discard the hard beak found at the
base of the tentacles. ❧

SHRIMP POPS ON SUGARCANE

I first encountered this charming dish

at A Touch of Saigon, a restaurant

in the unlikely setting of Wailuku

on the Hawaiian island of Maui.

Since the shrimp were presented

to resemble lollipops, the dish was

listed in English as shrimp pops.

In its homeland, the shrimp paste is

traditionally wrapped around the

center of the sugarcane stick, creating

handles on each end. But no matter

how you fashion it, the taste is

sensational.

Although the sugarcane stick is not

meant to be eaten, it can be sucked

for its sweet juice. If you can't locate

fresh or canned sugarcane in a local

market, substitute lemongrass stalks

or well-soaked wooden chopsticks,

form the shrimp mixture into small

Peanut Sauce, Vietnamese Style (page 152)

ACCOMPANIMENTS
3 ounces very thin, wiry dried rice noodles (vermicelli)
About 12 tender lettuce leaves, washed, dried, wrapped, and chilled to crisp
1 cup daikon matchsticks or slices
1 cup carrot matchsticks or slices
1 cup cucumber slices
1 cup mung bean sprouts
1 cup fresh mint leaves or sprigs
1 cup fresh Asian basil leaves or sprigs
1 cup fresh cilantro (coriander) leaves or sprigs
1 cup unsalted dry-roasted peanuts

SHRIMP PASTE
3 ounces bacon, coarsely chopped
1 pound shrimp
½ cup coarsely chopped shallot
3 tablespoons coarsely chopped garlic
1 tablespoon fish sauce
1 tablespoon sugar
1 teaspoon freshly ground black pepper, or to taste

Vegetable oil for moistening hands and brushing on grill rack
Fresh, canned, or preserved sugarcane, cut into 12 sticks each about 6 inches long and ½ inch in diameter
12 or more round rice paper wrappers (Vietnamese *bahn trang*), each about 8 inches in diameter
Fresh mint sprigs for garnish
Fresh Asian basil sprigs for garnish

Prepare the Peanut Sauce, Vietnamese Style as directed and set aside.

To prepare the accompaniments, first prepare the noodles as directed on page 159. Drain well before serving. Prepare the other accompaniments and refrigerate all except the peanuts until serving time. Set the peanuts aside.

To prepare the shrimp paste, combine the bacon with cold water to cover in a saucepan. Bring to a boil over medium-high heat and boil for about 5 minutes. Drain and transfer to a food processor or blender.

Peel and devein the shrimp, quickly rinse under cold running water, and pat dry with paper toweling. Transfer to the food processor or blender with the bacon. Add the shallot, garlic, fish sauce, sugar, and pepper. Process until a smooth paste is formed.

Recipe continues on page 80

78

balls and thread onto well-soaked

bamboo skewers, or simply shape the

mixture into patties and forget the

sticks. ❧

Prepare a grill for hot direct-heat cooking or preheat a broiler.

Moisten your hands with vegetable oil to prevent sticking and wrap about 2 tablespoons of the shrimp mixture around one end of each sugarcane stick, to resemble a lollipop.

When the fire or broiler is ready, lightly brush the grill or broiler rack with vegetable oil. Place the shrimp pops on the rack and grill or broil, turning occasionally, until the shrimp mixture is opaque throughout when tested by cutting with a small, sharp knife, about 8 minutes in all.

While the shrimp pops are cooking, arrange the chilled accompaniments and rice paper wrappers in bowls and/or on a large platter and place on the table. Spoon the peanut sauce into 6 small bowls, divide the chopped peanuts among 6 additional small bowls, and fill 6 wide, shallow bowls with hot water and position at each place.

Transfer the shrimp pops to a serving platter or divide among 6 individual plates and garnish with mint and basil sprigs.

To eat, dip a rice paper wrapper into the warm water until softened, then spread out on a plate. Slide the shrimp pop off the sugarcane onto the center of the softened wrapper. Add accompaniments as desired. Fold the bottom of the wrapper up around the filling, tuck in each side to encase the filling and then roll up to form a cylinder. Dip into the sauce en route to your mouth.

Makes 6 servings.

FISH IN LIME SAUCE

1½ pounds firm-fleshed or flaky-fleshed lean white fish fillet, skinned and
    cut into 8 equal pieces

MARINADE
3 tablespoons minced fresh galanga or ginger
3 tablespoons minced fresh or thawed frozen kaffir lime leaves
2 tablespoons minced fresh lemongrass, tender bulb portion only
2 tablespoons minced or pressed garlic
2 teaspoons ground turmeric

LIME SAUCE
2 tablespoons fish sauce
2 tablespoons soy sauce
2 cups water
4 tablespoons minced fresh galanga or ginger
2 tablespoons minced fresh lemongrass, tender bulb portion only
1 tablespoon minced fresh or thawed frozen kaffir lime leaves
3 tablespoons freshly squeezed lime juice
1 tablespoon palm sugar

8 ounces mung bean noodles
Boiling water
Canola oil or other high-quality vegetable oil for deep-frying
Rice flour or all-purpose flour for dredging
Fresh cilantro (coriander) sprigs for garnish
Lime slices for garnish

Quickly rinse the fish under cold running water, then pat dry with paper toweling;
set aside.

To make the marinade, in a bowl, combine all of the ingredients and mix well. Rub
the marinade over the entire surface of the fish and place in a shallow bowl or heavy-
duty lock-top plastic bag. Cover or seal securely and refrigerate for at least 2 hours
or as long as overnight.

To make the Lime Sauce, in a saucepan, combine the fish sauce, soy sauce, water,
galanga or ginger, lemongrass, and lime leaves. Place over medium-high heat and
bring to a boil. Reduce the heat to maintain a simmer and cook, stirring occasionally,
until the mixture is very flavorful, about 20 minutes. Add the lime juice and sugar
and stir until the sugar is dissolved, about 2 minutes. Strain into a bowl and set
aside.

Meanwhile, place the noodles in a bowl, cover with boiling water, and let stand
until softened but still firm to the bite, about 25 minutes. Drain well and set aside.

Recipe continues on page 83

TREI CHIEN
KROEUNG
· · ·
Cambodian

FISH IN LIME SAUCE

*C*atfish is commonly used in this
specialty of Cambodia, although just
about any fish will do, except those
with soft flesh, which would fall apart
during the double cooking. Ask your
local fish supplier for a fresh fish that
would be suitable for frying.

Although nontraditional, the well-
seasoned fried fish is also good served
without simmering it in the sauce.
Offer it with any one of the dipping
sauces on pages 146-148.

81

In a wok, deep-fat fryer, or large, deep pan such as a dutch oven, pour in oil to a depth of 2 inches. Heat to 375° F, or until a small piece of bread dropped into the hot oil turns golden brown within about 30 seconds. Preheat an oven to 200° F. Place a wire rack over a baking sheet; set aside.

Dredge the fish in flour to coat lightly all over, shaking off excess flour. Carefully immerse the fish, a few pieces at a time, into the hot oil; avoid crowding the pan. Cook, turning occasionally, until golden brown all over, about 5 minutes. Using a slotted utensil, remove the fish to the wire rack to drain well. Cook the remaining fish in the same manner, allowing the oil to return to 375° F between batches.

Pour the reserved lime sauce into a wok or skillet. Place over medium heat and bring to a boil, then reduce the heat to maintain a simmer. Add the fish and noodles and simmer, turning several times, until heated through.

To serve, using tongs or a pasta server, transfer the noodles to a large shallow bowl or distribute among 4 individual bowls. Arrange the fish over the noodles. Garnish with the cilantro sprigs and lime slices.

Makes 4 servings.

TOD MAN
Thai

FISH CAKES

*C*hoose cod, red snapper, salmon, sole, or other fish with flaky flesh for these patties.

For a refreshing treat, wrap the fish cakes in lettuce leaves with fresh mint or basil leaves, Vietnamese style, and eat out of hand after dipping into the sauce. ❧

FISH CAKES

Spicy Fish Dipping Sauce (page 148)
2 tablespoons Red Curry Paste (page 142) or canned Thai red curry paste, or to taste
2 pounds flaky-fleshed fish fillet (see recipe introduction), skinned and coarsely chopped
2 tablespoons cornstarch
1 egg, lightly beaten
2 tablespoons minced fresh or thawed frozen kaffir lime leaves
2 tablespoons fish sauce
1 tablespoon sugar
½ teaspoon freshly ground black or white pepper
Canola oil or other high-quality vegetable oil for deep-frying
Diced cucumber for garnish
Slivered green onion for garnish

Prepare the Spicy Fish Dipping Sauce as directed and set aside.

If using Red Curry Paste, prepare as directed and set aside. If using canned curry paste, reserve for later use.

Quickly rinse the fish under cold running water and pat dry with paper toweling.

In a food processor, blender, or heavy mortar with a pestle, combine the fish, curry paste, cornstarch, egg, minced lime leaves, fish sauce, sugar, and pepper and blend until the mixture forms a thick paste. Transfer to a bowl, cover, and refrigerate until chilled, 30 minutes to 1 hour.

In a wok, deep-fat fryer, or large, deep pan such as a dutch oven, pour in oil to a depth of 2 inches. Heat to 375° F, or until a small piece of bread dropped into the hot oil turns golden brown within about 30 seconds. Preheat an oven to 200° F. Place a wire rack over a baking sheet; set aside.

Meanwhile, using your hands, divide the chilled fish mixture into 12 equal portions and form each portion into a patty about 3 inches in diameter and ½ to ¾ inch thick.

Carefully immerse the patties, a few at a time, into the hot oil; avoid crowding the pan. Cook until golden brown on all sides, 5 to 6 minutes in all. Using a slotted utensil, remove the patties to the wire rack to drain well, then place in the preheated oven to keep warm. Cook the remaining fish patties in the same manner, allowing the oil to return to 375° F between batches.

Arrange the patties on a serving dish, sprinkle with cucumber and green onion, and serve warm with the dipping sauce.

Makes 4 to 6 servings.

GRILLED FISH WITH RED CURRY SAUCE

1¼ cups chilled Fresh Coconut Milk (page 140) or unshaken canned coconut milk
3 tablespoons Red Curry Paste (page 142) or canned Thai red curry paste, or to taste
2 pounds fish fillet (see recipe introduction), cut into 4 equal pieces
Salt
2 teaspoons fish sauce, or to taste
2 teaspoons soy sauce, or to taste
1 teaspoon palm sugar, or to taste
Vegetable oil for brushing wire basket or grill rack
Slivered green onion tops for garnish

If using Fresh Coconut Milk, prepare as directed and refrigerate until chilled. If using canned coconut milk, reserve for later use.

If using Red Curry Paste, prepare as directed and set aside. If using canned curry paste, reserve for later use.

Quickly rinse the fish under cold running water and pat dry with paper toweling. Measure the fish at the thickest point and note the measurement. Season to taste with salt and rub about 1½ tablespoons of the curry paste over the entire surface of the fish. Cover and refrigerate for at least 4 hours or as long as overnight; return the fish to room temperature just before cooking.

Prepare an open grill for hot direct-heat cooking.

Scoop ¼ cup of the coconut cream from the top of the chilled fresh or canned coconut milk and transfer to a small saucepan. Place over medium heat and bring to a boil. Stir in the remaining 1½ tablespoons of the curry paste and cook, stirring constantly, until very fragrant, about 5 minutes.

Stir the remaining 1 cup coconut milk to achieve a smooth consistency, then slowly stir it into the curry paste mixture. Add the fish sauce, soy sauce, and sugar. Bring to a boil, stirring constantly, then adjust the heat to maintain a simmer and cook, stirring frequently, until thickened to a thin sauce consistency, about 10 minutes. Taste and adjust with fish sauce, soy sauce, and palm sugar. Keep warm.

When the fire is ready, lightly brush the inside surface of a hinged wire basket with oil and place the fish inside, or brush the grill rack with oil. Place the fish in the basket and set on the grill rack or place the fish directly on the rack. Grill the fish, turning once, until the flesh is opaque when cut into at the thickest part with a small, sharp knife, about 10 minutes per inch of thickness, or until done to preference; avoid overcooking. Transfer to a cutting surface and remove any skin.

Pool the sauce onto a serving dish or divide evenly among 4 individual plates, top with the fish, and scatter the green onion over the top. Serve warm.

Makes 4 servings.

PLAH YAHNG GAENG PEHT
•••
Thai

GRILLED FISH WITH RED CURRY SAUCE

Although any fish may be grilled, those with soft flesh, such as sole, have a tendency to fall apart when they are turned. For this preparation, I prefer salmon, sea bass, catfish, or swordfish, but choose whatever is freshest at the market. ❧

Kai Toon
...
Thai

STEAMED SAVORY CUSTARD

*T*o make banana-leaf cups for the custard, cut fresh or thawed frozen banana leaves into 7-inch squares. For each cup, stack 2 squares with shiny sides facing up, then top with a saucer or bowl that fits almost to the edges of the squares. Using a small, sharp knife or scissors, cut around the saucer or bowl to form banana-leaf rounds. Gather the edges of one of the double-layered circles with your fingers to create a pleat and, using a hand-held stapler, fasten the leaves together about 1 inch from the edge to form a square corner. Fold and staple the opposite side of the circle in the same manner, then repeat the procedure on opposite sides of the round halfway between the first two pleats to form a square container. ❧

STEAMED SAVORY CUSTARD

Instead of the suggested shellfish, add cooked fish or ground or minced pork or chicken to the egg mixture. Or omit both the shellfish and meat for a silken Thai side dish.

4 eggs
1½ cups homemade chicken stock or fish stock or canned reduced-sodium chicken broth
2 tablespoons fish sauce
¾ teaspoon freshly ground white pepper
¾ cup flaked cooked crab meat or chopped cooked lobster
2 tablespoons minced green onion, including green tops
6 small to medium-sized shrimp, peeled and deveined
18 fine julienne strips sweet red pepper or fresh red hot chile

To prepare for steaming, position a rack in a wok or pan that will be large enough to hold six custard cups or banana-leaf cups (see recipe introduction for instructions) and can be completely covered by a lid. Pour in water to a level just below the steaming rack and place over high heat. Bring to a boil, then lower the heat to achieve a simmer.

In a bowl, crack the eggs and beat lightly with a fork until as smooth as possible; avoid overbeating at any point to prevent too many air bubbles from forming. Add the stock or broth, fish sauce, and pepper and gently blend until smooth. Strain the mixture through a fine-mesh sieve into a pitcher and set aside.

Spoon 2 tablespoons of the crab meat or lobster and 1 teaspoon of the onion into each of six 6-ounce custard cups or banana-leaf cups. Carefully pour the egg mixture over the crab meat or lobster and onion, distributing evenly among the cups.

Place the custard cups on the steamer rack. Wrap the lid of the steamer with several layers of paper toweling or a clean kitchen towel to prevent condensation from dripping on the custards, then cover the steamer. Steam until the custards are partially set, about 5 minutes, then remove the lid and place a shrimp and 3 strips of red pepper or chile on top of each custard. Cover and continue steaming until a knife inserted into the custard comes out clean, about 10 minutes longer; adjust the heat to maintain simmering water and continuous steam throughout cooking, adding boiling water if needed to maintain water level. Remove the steamer from the heat and uncover, being careful not to allow any condensation to drip onto the custards, then transfer the cups to a countertop to cool slightly.

Serve warm or at room temperature.

Makes 6 servings.

GAI TOTE
... Thai

FRIED CHICKEN WINGS

*T*hai cooks are famous for their fried stuffed chicken wings, known to American patrons of Thai restaurants as angel wings. They are wonderful to eat yet highly labor intensive to make, since the wings must be boned before stuffing. I discovered this simplified chicken wing dish at Bangkok Restaurant in Pleasant Hill, California, where Auntie Naila always orders them, along with jasmine rice and extra sauce, for eating as an American-style appetizer. Our little group of regular diners there have become quite addicted to them.

If you wish, substitute 16 chicken wing drummettes (large wing joints) for the whole wings. ◗

90

Sweet Chile-Garlic Dipping Sauce (page 146)
8 chicken wings
Salt
Canola oil or other high-quality vegetable oil for deep-frying
Rice flour for dusting
Finely chopped green onion, including green tops, for garnish

Prepare the Sweet Chile-Garlic Dipping Sauce as directed and set aside.

Quickly rinse the chicken wings under cold running water, then pat dry with paper toweling. Cut each wing at the two joints; reserve the tips for making stock. Lightly sprinkle the 16 wing pieces with salt and set aside.

In a wok, deep-fat fryer, or large, deep pan such as a dutch oven, pour in oil to a depth of 2 inches. Heat to 375° F, or until a small piece of bread dropped into the hot oil turns golden brown within about 30 seconds. Preheat an oven to 200° F. Place a wire rack over a baking sheet; set aside.

While the oil is heating, lightly dust the chicken pieces all over with rice flour, shaking off any excess flour.

Carefully immerse the chicken wings, a few at a time, into the hot oil; avoid crowding the pan. Cook until crispy and golden brown all over, about 10 minutes. Using a slotted utensil, remove the wings to the wire rack to drain well, then place in the preheated oven to keep warm. Cook the remaining wings in the same manner, allowing the oil to return to 375° F between batches.

To serve, arrange the chicken wings on a serving dish, spoon the sauce over them, and sprinkle with green onion.

Makes 4 servings.

VEGETARIAN VARIATION
Fried Tofu. Use 1 pound firm fresh tofu in place of the chicken. Drain well, cut into bite-sized cubes, lightly dust with rice flour, and deep-fry until golden brown, about 5 minutes.

GAI YAHNG
...
Thai

GRILLED CHICKEN

Succulent grilled chicken, which usually appears as barbecued chicken on menus in American Thai restaurants, is marinated in a spiced coconut mixture before it goes on the grill. ❧

92

GRILLED CHICKEN

¾ cup Fresh Coconut Milk (page 140) or shaken canned coconut milk
One 2½- to 3-pound frying chicken, cut into serving pieces, or 2 poussins (young chickens) or Cornish hens, split in half
2 tablespoons minced or pressed garlic
3 tablespoons minced fresh cilantro (coriander), preferably roots or lower stem portions
2 tablespoons fish sauce
1 tablespoon soy sauce, preferably dark Chinese style
1 teaspoon ground turmeric
1 teaspoon sugar
½ teaspoon freshly ground white pepper
Sweet Chile-Garlic Dipping Sauce (page 146)
Vegetable oil for brushing grill rack
Fresh cilantro (coriander) sprigs for garnish

If using Fresh Coconut Milk, prepare as directed and set aside. If using canned coconut milk, reserve for later use.

Quickly rinse the chicken under cold running water and pat dry with paper toweling.

In a bowl, combine the coconut milk, garlic, cilantro, fish sauce, soy sauce, turmeric, sugar, and pepper; mix well. Add the chicken and turn to coat on all sides. Cover and refrigerate, turning the chicken several times, for at least 4 hours or, preferably, overnight.

Prepare the Sweet Chile-Garlic Dipping Sauce as directed and set aside.

Prepare a covered grill for moderate indirect-heat cooking.

When the fire is ready, lightly brush the grill rack with vegetable oil. Remove the chicken from the marinade, reserving the marinade. Place the chicken on the rack and cook for 2 minutes to sear. Turn and cook on the second side for 2 minutes to sear. Cover the grill and cook, turning and brushing with the marinade every 6 to 7 minutes, until the juices run clear when the chicken is pierced with a fork near the joint, about 30 minutes in all.

Remove from the grill rack. If desired, place on a cutting surface and, using a heavy cleaver, chop into small pieces.

To serve, distribute the sauce among 4 individual bowls for dipping and position at each place, or transfer to a serving bowl for passing and spooning over the chicken at the table. Arrange the chicken on a serving platter or on 4 individual plates and garnish with cilantro sprigs.

Makes 4 servings.

LEMONGRASS CHICKEN

4 boned and skinned chicken breast halves
2 tablespoons minced fresh lemongrass, tender bulb portion only
3 green onions, including green tops, cut into 1-inch lengths, then
    thinly slivered
1 tablespoon slivered fresh red hot chile
1 tablespoon minced or pressed garlic
2 tablespoons fish sauce
1 teaspoon soy sauce
2 teaspoons sugar
½ teaspoon freshly ground black pepper
3 tablespoons canola oil or other high-quality vegetable oil
Shredded fresh mint leaves for garnish
Lemongrass stalk for garnish (optional)
Fresh mint sprigs for garnish (optional)

Quickly rinse the chicken under cold running water and pat dry with paper
toweling. Cut into bite-sized pieces.

In a bowl, combine the chicken, minced lemongrass, onions, chile, garlic, fish
sauce, soy sauce, sugar and pepper and toss well to coat the chicken. Cover and
refrigerate for 1 to 3 hours. Return to room temperature before cooking.

Place a wok, large sauté pan, or large, heavy skillet over high heat. When the
pan is hot, add the oil and swirl to coat the pan. When the oil is hot but not yet
smoking, add the chicken mixture and stir-fry, moving the pan off and on the
heat as necessary to prevent scorching, until the chicken turns opaque throughout,
about 3 minutes; to check for doneness, cut into a piece with a small, sharp knife.

Transfer to a serving platter, sprinkle with mint, garnish with lemongrass stalk and
mint sprigs (if using), and serve warm.

Makes 4 servings.

GA XAO
Vietnamese

LEMONGRASS CHICKEN

*F*resh lemongrass is essential for this
simple dish from Vietnam. For easier
and healthier dining, I've used boned
and skinned chicken breasts instead
of the usual whole chicken, which is
traditionally cut up on the bone. ❧

RAMARONGSONG GAI PAHT
· · ·
Thai

ROYAL SWIMMING CHICKEN

Sometimes translated as "rama-a-swimming" or "rama-a-bathing," here is one of those unusually named Thai dishes. Rama means "king," indicating that the dish was probably created in the royal palace, and rongsong describes bathing or swimming, referring to the chicken floating over a green "sea." I've also been served this same preparation under the name swimming angel. In any case, it is quick, easy, and tasty.

Lush, green swamp cabbage (pug boong or pak bung in Thai and kangkung in Indonesian and Malaysian), also known as water spinach, convolvulus, and morning glory, is sometimes available by one of its many names in Asian markets. Spinach is an excellent substitute. ❧

1 cup Fresh Coconut Milk (page 140) or shaken canned coconut milk
½ cup Peanut Sauce, Thai Style (page 150)
About 4 quarts water
1 tablespoon salt
2 pounds fresh swamp cabbage (see recipe introduction) or spinach, very well washed and any large stems discarded
1 pound boned and skinned chicken breasts
Finely chopped unsalted dry-roasted peanuts

If using Fresh Coconut Milk, prepare as directed and set aside. If using canned coconut milk, reserve for later use.

Prepare the Peanut Sauce, Thai Style as directed and set aside.

In a large pan, bring the water to a boil over medium-high heat. Stir in the salt. Add the swamp cabbage or spinach, return to a boil, and boil for about 2 minutes. Drain immediately in a colander set in a sink and rinse with cold water to halt the cooking and preserve the color. Press with your hands to remove excess water. Arrange as a bed on a serving platter; set aside.

Quickly rinse the chicken under cold running water and pat dry with paper toweling. Cut into long strips about ¼-inch wide and set aside.

In a wok or heavy saucepan over medium heat, bring the coconut milk to a gentle boil. Add the chicken, reduce the heat to very low, and barely simmer until the chicken just turns opaque, about 10 minutes; test by cutting into the chicken with a small, sharp knife. Using a slotted utensil, remove the chicken to the center of the spinach.

Add the peanut sauce to the coconut milk used for poaching the chicken. Place over medium-high heat and cook, stirring frequently, until the mixture is smooth and thickened, about 5 minutes. Pour over the chicken. Sprinkle with the peanuts and serve warm.

Makes 4 servings.

KAI LAO
...
Laotian

STUFFED CHICKEN

*O*n *special occasions, Laotian cooks stuff a large stewing chicken and simmer it in coconut milk until tender. I've adapted the idea, creating this quicker-cooking and easier-to-serve dish.*

Although any white rice may be used for this dish, sticky rice (page 18) is the starch of choice for all Laotian meals. To use it for stuffing, cook the rice just before stuffing the chicken with it and set aside the leftover rice to accompany the finished dish. The rice may be kept warm in the steamer or eaten at room temperature. Keep in mind that sticky rice must be soaked for at least 4 hours, or preferably overnight, before cooking. ❦

STUFFED CHICKEN

2 cups Fresh Coconut Milk (page 140) or unshaken canned coconut milk
Sticky Rice (page 18)

STUFFING
1 tablespoon canola oil or other high-quality vegetable oil
1 cup chopped shallot
1 tablespoon minced fresh galanga or ginger
1 teaspoon minced or pressed garlic
1 tablespoon minced fresh red or green hot chile
4 ounces ground lean pork
2 tablespoons minced fresh cilantro (coriander)
Salt
Freshly ground black pepper

8 boned and skinned chicken breast halves
12 tops from green onions, blanched in hot water to soften (optional)
2 tablespoons fish sauce, or to taste
Fresh cilantro (coriander) sprigs for garnish

If using Fresh Coconut Milk, prepare as directed and refrigerate until chilled. If using canned coconut milk, reserve for later use.

Prepare the Sticky Rice as directed. Cover and set aside.

To make the stuffing, place a wok, large sauté pan, or heavy skillet over high heat. When the pan is hot, add the oil and swirl to coat the pan. When the oil is hot but not yet smoking, add the shallot and galanga or ginger and stir-fry until soft, about 1 minute. Add the garlic and chile and stir-fry about 30 seconds longer. Add the pork and stir-fry, moving the pan off and on the heat as necessary to prevent scorching, until the meat is opaque, about 2 minutes longer. Remove from the heat and drain off and discard any rendered fat from the pork.

Scoop ½ cup of the coconut cream from the top of the chilled fresh or canned coconut milk and stir into the stuffing mixture. Add ½ cup of the rice, the cilantro, and salt and pepper to taste and blend well. Set aside to cool while you prepare the chicken.

Quickly rinse the chicken under cold running water and pat dry with paper toweling. Discard tendons and any connective tissue or fat from the chicken breasts; separate the little fillet and use it for another purpose or leave it attached and tuck it under the larger muscle. Place each breast between 2 sheets of waxed paper or plastic wrap and pound with a meat mallet or other flat instrument to a uniform thickness of about ⅛ inch. Lightly sprinkle both sides with salt and pepper.

Spoon about 3 tablespoons of the stuffing onto the center of each piece of pounded chicken. Roll up the chicken to encase the filling and tie with green onion strips (if using) or cotton string to form a bundle, or secure lengthwise with a skewer or toothpicks.

Recipe continues on page 100

Place the chicken rolls in a large flat pan. Stir the remaining 1½ cups coconut milk to achieve a smooth consistency and pour it, along with the fish sauce, evenly over the chicken. Place over medium heat and bring to a simmer, then cover and reduce the heat to keep the liquid barely simmering. Cook, turning frequently, until the chicken is tender and has just turned opaque all the way through when cut into with a small, sharp knife, 12 to 15 minutes.

Remove the chicken to a serving dish. Increase the heat under the cooking liquid and boil until reduced to a thin sauce consistency, about 8 minutes; strain to remove any bits of filling if desired. Pour the sauce over the chicken, garnish with cilantro sprigs, and serve warm or at room temperature.

Makes 8 servings.

THAI CURRY

2½ cups Fresh Coconut Milk (page 140) or unshaken canned coconut milk
2 tablespoons Red, Green, or Yellow Curry Paste (pages 142, 143, or 144)
  or canned Thai red, green, or yellow curry paste, or to taste
1 pound boned and skinned chicken or boneless tender beef, lamb, or pork;
  or 2 cups cut-up roasted or barbecued boned duck; or 1 pound fresh fish
  fillet or peeled shellfish
3 tablespoons fish sauce, or to taste
1 tablespoon palm sugar, or to taste
¾ cup sliced canned bamboo shoots
¾ cup fresh, thawed frozen, or drained canned corn kernels
1 sweet red pepper, seeds and membranes discarded, then sliced lengthwise
  into thin strips
6 tiny fresh red or green hot chiles, preferably Thai bird variety, or to taste;
  or 3 larger fresh red or green hot chiles, such as serrano, or to taste, seeds
  and membranes discarded, sliced lengthwise into quarters
¾ cup fresh Asian basil leaves
6 fresh or thawed frozen kaffir lime leaves (optional)
2 tablespoons freshly squeezed lime juice, or to taste

If using Fresh Coconut Milk, prepare as directed and refrigerate until chilled. If using canned coconut milk, reserve for later use.

If using homemade curry paste, prepare the selected curry paste as directed and set aside. If using canned curry paste, reserve for later use.

If using chicken, quickly rinse under cold running water, pat dry with paper toweling, and cut into bite sized pieces; set aside. If using meat, quickly rinse under cold running water, pat dry with paper toweling, slice across the grain as thinly as possible, and cut each slice into pieces about 2 inches long by ½ inch wide; set aside. If using cooked duck, set aside. If using fish or shellfish, quickly rinse under cold running water, pat dry with paper toweling, and cut fish or large shellfish into bite-sized pieces; set aside.

Scoop ½ cup of the coconut cream from the top of the chilled fresh or canned coconut milk and transfer to a wok or heavy saucepan. Place over medium heat and bring to a boil. Stir in the curry paste and cook, stirring constantly, until very fragrant, about 5 minutes. If using chicken or meat, add it to the pan and cook, stirring frequently, until the meat is browned, about 5 minutes. If using cooked duck, add it to the pan and cook, stirring frequently, for about 1 minute.

Stir the remaining 2 cups coconut milk to achieve a smooth consistency, then slowly stir it into the pan. If using fish or shellfish, add it to the pan. Stir in the fish sauce and sugar. Add the bamboo shoots, corn, sweet pepper, chiles, ½ cup of the basil leaves, and the lime leaves (if using). Bring to a simmer and cook until the

Recipe continues on page 103

GAENG
•••
Thai

THAI CURRY

A big bowl of fragrant Thai curry

is guaranteed to thrill chile addicts.

This recipe is a guide to the basic

method for making curry. It can be

greatly varied by using a rainbow of

Thai curry pastes, a range of meats

or fish, and whatever vegetables are

appealing. A particularly delicious

version, shown in the photograph,

is made with roasted or barbecued

duck, available whole from Chinese

markets or restaurants or cooked at

home.

Contrary to popular opinion, not all

curries need to be rich with coconut

milk in order to be flavorful. To

reduce the amount of calorie-laden

coconut milk, use one of the thinner

variations of coconut milk (page 141)

or blend some coconut milk with

chicken or meat is done, 5 to 15 minutes, depending on type; or until the duck is heated through, about 5 minutes; or until the fish or shellfish turn opaque, about 5 minutes. Stir in the lime juice. Taste and adjust the fish sauce, sugar, and lime juice to achieve a good balance of salty, sweet, and sour.

Ladle into a serving bowl and stir in the remaining ¼ cup basil leaves. Serve warm.

Makes 4 servings.

VEGETARIAN VARIATION
Use 1 pound firm tofu, tempeh (firm fermented bean curd), or eggplant or other vegetables, cut into bite-sized cubes, in place of the meat and cook until tender. If using vegetables that cook at different times, start with those that require the longest cooking and add quicker-cooking vegetables near the end. Substitute 1½ tablespoons soy sauce for the fish sauce.

flavorful stock to equal the amount of liquid called for in the recipe. To prepare a noncoconut curry, fry the curry paste in vegetable oil, then substitute water, a light broth, or a combination of water and stock for the coconut milk. ❧

GA NUONG BUN
Vietnamese

GRILLED SKEWERED CHICKEN
WITH NOODLES

Although this skewered specialty from Vietnam tastes great when served, as Indonesian sate or Thai satay, with a dipping sauce, it is more intriguing when offered, as shown here, in a meal-in-a-bowl presentation. The dish, known as bun or bahn style because of the noodles, may also be prepared from beef, pork, shrimp, or meatballs.

Alternatively, the grilled tidbits can be offered on a tray with lettuce leaves, bean sprouts, mint or other fragrant herb leaves, and thin strips of carrot, cucumber, and chile. Diners slip the meat off the skewers onto a lettuce leaf, add selected accompaniments, roll up the leaf, and dip the packet into the sauce before eating. ❧

GRILLED SKEWERED CHICKEN WITH NOODLES

MARINADE
¼ cup fish sauce
¼ cup freshly squeezed lime juice
2 tablespoons soy sauce
2 tablespoons canola oil or other high-quality vegetable oil
1 tablespoon palm sugar

4 boned and skinned chicken breast halves
Chile Dipping Sauce, Vietnamese Style (page 147) or Sweet Chile-Garlic Dipping Sauce (page 146)
8 ounces very thin, wiry dried rice noodles (vermicelli)
Vegetable oil for brushing grill rack or broiler pan
1 cup mung bean sprouts
½ cup chopped or shredded crisp lettuce such as romaine
½ cup chopped or shredded fresh mint
½ cup shredded carrot
½ cup shredded cucumber
½ cup julienned or minced red hot chile
½ cup chopped unsalted dry-roasted peanuts
Lime wedges for serving

To make the marinade, in a bowl, combine all the ingredients, mix well, and set aside.

Quickly rinse the chicken under cold running water and pat dry with paper toweling. Cut into bite-sized pieces, place in the marinade, cover, and refrigerate for at least 2 hours or, preferably, overnight.

Prepare the selected dipping sauce as directed and set aside.

About 30 minutes before cooking, place 12 bamboo skewers in a shallow container, cover with water, and set aside to soak. Prepare an open grill for moderate direct-heat cooking. Prepare the noodles as directed on page 159 and let stand in cold water until serving time.

Remove the chicken from the marinade, reserving the marinade, and thread onto the skewers.

When the fire is ready, lightly brush the grill rack with oil. Place the skewered chicken on the rack and grill, turning frequently and basting with the marinade, until opaque throughout, about 6 minutes.

To serve, distribute the dipping sauce among 4 small bowls and set at each place. Drain the noodles and divide evenly among 4 large, shallow soup bowls. Scatter equal portions of the bean sprouts, lettuce, mint, carrot, cucumber, chile, and peanuts over the top of each portion of noodles. Arrange 3 chicken skewers on top of each serving and place lime wedges alongside. Each diner may pour the sauce over the chicken and noodles or use it for dipping.

Makes 4 servings.

SATE
Indonesian and Malaysian
SATAY
Thai

GRILLED SKEWERED MEAT

Sate is a specialty of Indonesia and Malaysia that has spread throughout tropical Asia. Pork is taboo among followers of the Islam religion, but is popular with Southeast Asians of other beliefs, so I've included it among the meats of choice. This recipe is merely an example of the countless versions sold by street vendors or prepared by home cooks from Myanmar to Bali.

In addition to the meats and chicken suggested in the recipe, meatballs, shrimp, chunks of fish, or firm tofu cubes are excellent prepared this way.

Cucumber Relish (page 154) is a traditional Thai accompaniment. ❧

GRILLED SKEWERED MEAT

Select the creamy Peanut Sauce, Indonesian Style; the spicier Peanut Sauce, Thai Style; or the Chinese-inspired Peanut Sauce, Vietnamese Style to accompany the skewered meat. Or for a change of pace, omit the ground peanuts or peanut butter from the marinade and serve the grilled meat with Sweet Chile-Garlic Dipping Sauce (page 146) or Chile Dipping Sauce, Vietnamese Style (page 147) in place of the peanut sauce.

12 ounces boneless lean beef, lamb, or pork or boned and skinned chicken breast

MARINADE
1 tablespoon Red Curry Paste (page 142) or canned Thai red curry paste
1 tablespoon palm sugar
2 tablespoons finely ground unsalted dry-roasted peanuts or peanut butter
¼ cup fish sauce
¼ cup freshly squeezed lime juice
1 teaspoon minced fresh lemongrass, tender bulb portion only
1 teaspoon minced or pressed garlic

Peanut sauce (pages 150-152; see recipe introduction)
Vegetable oil for brushing grill rack or broiler pan

Quickly rinse the meat or chicken under cold running water and pat dry with paper toweling. To facilitate slicing, wrap the meat or chicken in freezer wrap or plastic wrap and place in a freezer until very cold but not frozen hard, about 2 hours.

To make the marinade, if using Red Curry Paste, prepare as directed. In a bowl, combine all the marinade ingredients, mix well, and set aside.

Using an electric slicer or very sharp knife, slice the meat or chicken very thinly, then cut into strips from 3 to 4 inches long and about 1 inch wide. Place in the marinade, cover, and refrigerate for at least 2 hours or, preferably, overnight.

Prepare the selected peanut sauce as directed and set aside.

About 30 minutes before cooking, place 8 to 10 bamboo skewers in a shallow container, cover with water, and set aside to soak. Prepare an open grill for moderate direct-heat cooking.

Remove the meat or chicken pieces from the marinade, reserving the marinade, and thread onto the skewers, weaving the skewers in and out of the meat and using 2 pieces per skewer.

When the fire is ready, lightly brush the grill rack with oil. Place the skewered meat or chicken on the rack and grill, turning frequently and basting with the marinade, until done, 4 to 5 minutes. Transfer to a serving platter and serve warm with the peanut sauce.

Makes 4 servings.

KANOM PANG NA MOO
Thai

THAI TOAST

*A*mong *the first words my nephew Devereux spoke were "Thai toast," his favorite dish at Swatdee restaurant in San Francisco, and among his earliest solid foods. All ages delight in this traditional snack.*

These little tidbits fry best at around 350° F; any hotter will brown them too quickly before the spread is done.

For Vietnamese Shrimp Toast (banh mi chien voi tom), prepare the mixture for Shrimp Pops on Sugarcane (page 78). Smear it over baguette slices and fry as directed. Serve with Peanut Sauce, Vietnamese Style (page 152). ❧

108

Peanut Sauce, Thai Style (page 150)
Cucumber Relish (page 154)
5 ounces ground lean pork
2½ tablespoons finely chopped green onion, including green tops
1 tablespoon finely chopped fresh cilantro (coriander), preferably roots
   or lower stem portions
1 teaspoon minced garlic
2 teaspoons fish sauce
1 egg, lightly beaten
1 teaspoon freshly ground white pepper
¼ teaspoon salt
About 6 slices stale, fine-textured white bread
Canola oil or other high-quality vegetable oil for deep-frying
Fresh cilantro (coriander) leaves for garnish
Thinly slivered sweet red pepper or red hot chile for garnish

Prepare the Peanut Sauce, Thai Style, and the Cucumber Relish as directed. Set each aside.

In a food processor or mixing bowl, combine the pork, onion, cilantro, garlic, fish sauce, egg, pepper, and salt and process or mix well with your hands until the mixture is thick and sticky. (At this point the mixture can be covered and refrigerated for up to 24 hours before assembling the toasts.)

Trim crusts from each slice of bread, then cut bread into 4 triangles or squares. Spread each piece of bread with an equal portion of the pork mixture, mounding the mixture slightly in the center and tapering toward the edges; be sure to spread the mixture all the way to the edges of the bread.

In a wok, deep-fat fryer, or large, deep pan such as a dutch oven, pour in oil to a depth of 2 inches. Heat to 350° F, or until a small piece of bread dropped into the hot oil turns golden brown within about 45 seconds. Preheat an oven to 200° F. Place a wire rack over a baking sheet; set aside.

Carefully add a few pieces of the bread, meat side down, to the hot oil; avoid overcrowding the pan. Cook until crisp and golden brown, about 1 minute, turning the toasts during the last 10 seconds to brown the bottom. Using a slotted utensil, remove the toasts to the wire rack, meat side down, to drain well, then place in the preheated oven to keep warm. Cook the remaining bread pieces in the same manner, allowing the oil to return to 350° F between batches.

Garnish each toast with a cilantro leaf and a sliver or two of sweet pepper or chile. Serve warm with the Cucumber Relish alongside and offer the peanut sauce at the table.

Makes 4 or 5 servings.

MINCED PORK ON PINEAPPLE

2 tablespoons Tamarind Liquid (page 156)
2 tablespoons chopped fresh cilantro (coriander), preferably roots
   or lower stem portions
1½ tablespoons minced or pressed garlic
¾ teaspoon black or white peppercorns
2 or 3 teaspoons canola oil or other high-quality vegetable oil
8 ounces minced or ground lean pork
3 tablespoons finely chopped unsalted dry-roasted peanuts
1 tablespoon minced fresh green or red hot chile
2½ tablespoons palm sugar
2 tablespoons fish sauce
1 small ripe pineapple
Red sweet pepper, cut into tiny dice, for garnish
Minced fresh cilantro (coriander) for garnish

Prepare the Tamarind Liquid as directed and set aside.

In a spice grinder, mini food processor, or heavy mortar with a pestle, grind the chopped cilantro, garlic, and peppercorns as finely as possible, adding 1 teaspoon of the oil if needed to facilitate grinding. Set aside.

In a wok or heavy sauté pan, heat 2 teaspoons oil over medium heat. Add the cilantro mixture and stir-fry until fragrant, 1 to 2 minutes. Add the pork and peanuts and stir-fry, breaking up the pork with the cooking utensil, until the meat loses its pink color, about 2 minutes.

Add the chile, sugar, fish sauce, and Tamarind Liquid and continue stir-frying until the meat is well browned and tender, about 5 minutes. The liquid should be reduced and the mixture fairly dry, and there will probably be some greenish oil separated from the mixture. Remove from the heat, strain off and discard any oil, pour into a bowl, and let cool to room temperature.

Peel the pineapple, then slice crosswise into 5 slices each about ¼ inch thick; use any remaining pineapple for another purpose. Cut each pineapple slice into 8 wedges, discarding the hard core from the center of the fruit if desired.

To serve, mound about 1 teaspoon of the pork mixture onto each pineapple wedge. Sprinkle with the sweet pepper and cilantro and arrange on a serving tray.

Makes about 40 pieces, enough for 10 servings.

VARIATION
Substitute minced or ground chicken for the pork.

MAH HAW
···
Thai

MINCED PORK ON PINEAPPLE

*N*ot one Thai food authority or reference book seems to have a logical explanation as to the origin of the name for this dish, which is commonly translated as "galloping horses." No matter what the name refers to, the combination is sensational and makes a welcome addition to the American appetizer repertoire or to any Southeast Asian meal.

For easier serving, mound the pork on a platter and surround with the pineapple wedges. Diners scoop the meat onto the fruit for eating. ◗

MOO GRATIEM
Thai

GARLIC PORK

*O*f *all the delectable Thai ways with pork, this simple preparation is my all-time favorite.*

This dish may also be prepared with chicken. ❧

GARLIC PORK

8 ounces boneless lean pork
2 tablespoons minced or pressed garlic
1 teaspoon freshly ground white pepper
3 tablespoons fish sauce
2 tablespoons oyster sauce
1 tablespoon palm sugar
2 tablespoons canola oil or other high-quality vegetable oil
¼ cup chopped shallot
Fresh cilantro (coriander) sprigs for garnish

Quickly rinse the pork under cold running water and pat dry with paper toweling. To facilitate slicing, wrap the pork in freezer wrap or plastic wrap and place in a freezer until very cold but not frozen hard, about 2 hours.

Using an electric slicer or very sharp knife, slice the pork across the grain as thinly as possible, then cut each slice into pieces about 2 inches long by ½ inch wide. In a bowl, combine the pork, garlic, and pepper and toss to mix well. Cover tightly and refrigerate for at least 1 hour or as long as overnight.

In a small bowl, combine the fish sauce, oyster sauce, and sugar and stir to dissolve the sugar; set aside.

Place a wok, large sauté pan, or large, heavy skillet over high heat. When the pan is hot, add the oil and swirl to coat the pan. When the oil is hot but not smoking, add the shallot and stir-fry for about 1 minute. Add the pork mixture and stir-fry, moving the pan off and on the heat as necessary to prevent scorching, until the meat is no longer pink, about 2 minutes. Add the fish sauce mixture and cook until the meat is well coated and the liquid thickens slightly, about 1 minute longer.

Remove from the heat and transfer to a serving platter. Garnish with cilantro sprigs and serve warm or at room temperature.

Makes 4 servings.

NAHN PRIK OHNG
· · ·
Thai

VOLCANIC PORK SAUCE WITH VEGETABLES

I've dubbed this "volcanic" due to the intense fire of the chiles and the molten lava appearance of the dip. Adjust the amount of chiles to your preference. About 4 teaspoons Red Chile Sauce (page 148) or bottled red chile sauce (Indonesian sambal ulek or Vietnamese tuong ot) may be substituted for the dried or fresh chiles.

The day before serving this dish, begin to prepare Sticky Rice (page 18), which is characteristically dipped into the pork along with the vegetables. Although Thais serve the pork dip with raw vegetables, often elaborately carved, I particularly enjoy it with grilled eggplant. If you wish to be authentic, offer crisply fried pork skins for dipping as well. ❧

2 tablespoons small dried red hot chiles, preferably Thai bird variety, or minced fresh red hot chile
3 tablespoons coarsely chopped shallot
1 tablespoon coarsely chopped garlic
¾ teaspoon bottled moist shrimp paste (Thai *ga-pi*)
2 tablespoons canola oil or other high-quality vegetable oil
6 ounces ground lean pork
1¼ cups peeled, seeded, drained, and chopped fresh or canned tomato, coarsely puréed in a food processor or blender
4 teaspoons fish sauce
1 teaspoon palm sugar
Salt

VEGETABLES FOR DIPPING
Green beans, blanched
Cucumber slices
Carrot slices or sticks
Jicama sticks
Baby corn ears, blanched
Zucchini or other summer squash slices or sticks
Cabbage wedges
Thai globe eggplants
Eggplant slices, roasted or grilled

If using dried chiles, discard the stems and shake out the seeds if desired. Place in a small bowl, add warm water to cover, and let stand until softened, about 20 minutes. Drain, reserving the soaking water.

Place the drained dried or fresh chiles in a mini food processor, blender, or heavy mortar with a pestle. Add the shallot, garlic, and shrimp paste. Blend to a thick paste, adding up to 2 tablespoons water or the chile soaking water if needed to facilitate blending.

Place a wok, large sauté pan, or large, heavy skillet over medium heat. When the pan is hot, add the oil and swirl to coat the pan. When the oil is hot, add the chile mixture and cook, stirring constantly, until fragrant, 2 to 3 minutes.

Increase the heat to medium-high and add the pork. Stir-fry until the pork loses its pink color, breaking up the meat with the cooking utensil. Stir in the tomato and cook, stirring frequently, until most of the liquid has evaporated, about 10 minutes. Add the fish sauce, sugar, and salt to taste and cook, stirring frequently, until the liquid has evaporated, about 4 minutes. Remove from the heat and drain off and discard any rendered fat from the pork.

To serve, transfer the pork sauce to a small bowl placed on a serving plate or in a shallow basket and arrange the selected vegetables alongside.

Makes 6 servings.

NUEA PAD PRIK
Thai

CHILE BEEF WITH FRAGRANT HERBS

As with all stir-fried dishes, be sure to prepare all the ingredients in advance of cooking and arrange in small bowls alongside the stove.

This preparation is also wonderful when made with lamb. ◗

CHILE BEEF WITH FRAGRANT HERBS

12 ounces sirloin, flank, or other boneless tender lean beef
2 tablespoons fish sauce
2 tablespoons soy sauce
2 tablespoons oyster sauce
2 tablespoons palm sugar
¼ teaspoon freshly ground white pepper
2 tablespoons canola oil or other high-quality vegetable oil
½ cup thinly sliced shallot
1 tablespoon minced or pressed garlic
2 tablespoons minced fresh red or green hot chile, preferably Thai bird variety, or to taste
3 green onions, including green tops, cut into 1-inch lengths
½ cup fresh mint leaves
1 cup fresh Asian basil leaves
Fresh mint sprigs for garnish
Fresh Asian basil sprigs for garnish

Quickly rinse the beef under cold running water and pat dry with paper toweling. To facilitate slicing, wrap the beef in freezer wrap or plastic wrap and place in a freezer until very cold but not frozen hard, about 2 hours.

Using an electric slicer or very sharp knife, slice the beef across the grain as thinly as possible, then cut each slice into pieces about 2 inches long by ½ inch wide.

In a small bowl, combine the fish sauce, soy sauce, oyster sauce, sugar, and pepper and stir to dissolve the sugar; set aside.

Place a wok, large sauté pan, or large, heavy skillet over high heat. When the pan is hot, add the oil and swirl to coat the pan. When the oil is hot but not smoking, add the shallot and stir-fry for about 1 minute. Add the garlic and chile and stir-fry for about 30 seconds. Add the beef and stir-fry, moving the pan off and on the heat as necessary to prevent scorching, until the meat is barely past the pink stage, about 2 minutes.

Add the green onions, mint leaves, basil leaves, and the reserved fish sauce mixture; stir-fry until the leaves wilt and the meat is well coated with the sauce, about 2 minutes. Transfer to a serving dish, garnish with mint and basil sprigs, and serve warm or at room temperature.

Makes 4 servings.

Dry Beef Curry

1 cup Fresh Coconut Milk (page 140) or shaken canned coconut milk

SEASONING PASTE (INDONESIAN *BUMBU* OR MALAYSIAN *REMPAH*)
1 tablespoon Red Chile Sauce (page 148) or bottled red chile sauce
  (Indonesian *sambal ulek* or Vietnamese *tuong ot*)
2 cups coarsely chopped shallot
2 tablespoons coarsely chopped garlic
3 tablespoons sliced fresh lemongrass, tender bulb portion only
5 tablespoons coarsely chopped fresh galanga or ginger
1 tablespoon ground paprika

1½ pounds boneless beef (see recipe introduction)
¼ cup canola oil or other high-quality vegetable oil
12 fresh or thawed frozen kaffir lime leaves, finely slivered
About 2 tablespoons palm sugar
About 2 teaspoons salt
About 2 tablespoons freshly squeezed lime juice
Fresh pesticide-free lime or lemon leaves for garnish
Lime slices for garnish

If using Fresh Coconut Milk, prepare as directed and set aside. If using canned coconut milk, reserve for later use.

To make the seasoning paste, if using Red Chile Sauce, prepare as directed. In a food processor, blender, or heavy mortar with a pestle, combine the chile sauce, shallot, garlic, lemongrass, galanga or ginger, and paprika and blend to a thick paste, adding up to 3 tablespoons water if needed to facilitate blending. Set aside.

Trim the beef of excess fat. Quickly rinse the beef under cold running water and pat dry with paper toweling. Cut into 1-inch cubes. Set aside.

Place a wok, large sauté pan, or large, heavy skillet over medium heat. When the pan is hot, add the oil and swirl to coat the pan. When the oil is hot, add the seasoning paste and cook, stirring constantly, until the mixture is very fragrant and darker and the oil begins to separate from the paste, about 8 minutes.

Add the reserved beef, coconut milk, and slivered lime leaves. Adjust the heat so that the mixture barely simmers; do not allow it to boil. Simmer, uncovered and stirring occasionally, for about 45 minutes. Season to taste with sugar, salt, and lime juice. Continue to simmer until the meat is very tender, almost falling apart, and the sauce is thick and adheres to the beef, about 1½ hours longer; add a little hot water if the sauce becomes too thick. Taste and adjust the amount of sugar, salt, and lime juice to achieve a good balance of sweet, salty, and sour.

Transfer to a serving dish, garnish with lime or lemon leaves and lime slices, and serve warm.

Makes 6 servings.

RENDANG
Indonesian and Malaysian

DRY BEEF CURRY

Rendang *is a style of curry in which the sauce becomes a thick, dry coating that adheres to the meat. I use tender, lean beef such as sirloin or top round, which renders a succulent stew within a couple of hours. If you prefer to use stewing beef such as chuck or rump roast, increase the final simmering time to about 3 hours, adding a little more coconut milk or water as needed to keep the meat from drying out completely.*

Lamb makes a tasty substitute for the beef.

Golden Festival Rice (page 23) pairs perfectly with rendang.

GAENG MUSSAMUN
...
Thai

MUSLIM-STYLE CURRY

Like most stews, this dish, traditionally made with beef, improves in flavor when made a day ahead and slowly reheated before serving. Its name probably comes from the word Muslim and the spices used reflect the influence of Indian ingredients upon Thai cooking.

120

Chicken or lamb may be substituted for the beef, and vegetarians can enjoy this stew made with 2 pounds potatoes or a mixture of root vegetables such as carrots and turnips in place of the meat. Cook until the vegetables are done to preference and substitute about 2 tablespoons soy sauce for the fish sauce. ❧

5 cups Fresh Coconut Milk (page 140) or unshaken canned coconut milk
3 tablespoons Mussamun Curry Paste (page 145) or canned Thai *mussamun* curry paste
About 3 tablespoons Tamarind Liquid (page 156)
1 pound boneless beef for stewing, such as chuck or rump roast
About 3 tablespoons palm sugar
About 3 tablespoons fish sauce
½ cup unsalted dry-roasted peanuts
¼ teaspoon cardamom seeds, or 8 cardamom pods
2 cinnamon sticks, each about 3½ inches long
8 small pearl onions, peeled, or 1 large onion, cut lengthwise into 8 wedges
1 pound small new potatoes, peeled, or larger new potatoes, peeled and cut into 1-inch chunks
About 2 tablespoons freshly squeezed lime juice
Freshly slivered lime zest for garnish

If using Fresh Coconut Milk, prepare as directed and refrigerate until chilled. If using canned coconut milk, reserve for later use.

If using Mussamun Curry Paste, prepare as directed and set aside. If using canned curry paste, reserve for later use. Prepare the Tamarind Liquid as directed and set aside.

Trim the beef of excess fat. Quickly rinse the beef under cold running water, pat dry with paper toweling, and cut into 1-inch cubes. Set aside.

Scoop 1 cup of the coconut cream from the top of the chilled fresh or canned coconut milk and set aside. Stir the remaining coconut milk to achieve a smooth consistency and pour into a large saucepan. Place over medium heat and bring to a gentle boil.

Add the beef to the coconut milk, adjust the heat to maintain a simmer, and cook, uncovered and stirring occasionally, until the meat is just tender, 1 to 1½ hours.

Pour the reserved coconut cream into a wok, small sauté pan, or small, heavy skillet. Place over medium heat and bring to a boil. Stir in the curry paste and cook, stirring constantly, until very fragrant, about 5 minutes. Stir the curry paste mixture into the simmering coconut milk and beef.

Add 3 tablespoons *each* of the sugar, fish sauce, and Tamarind Liquid to the simmering curry. Stir in the peanuts, cardamom seeds or pods, cinnamon sticks, onions, and potatoes. Adjust the heat to achieve and maintain a simmer and cook, uncovered, stirring occasionally, until the potatoes are tender when pierced with a wooden skewer or small, sharp knife, about 20 minutes.

Stir in the lime juice. Taste and adjust with sugar, fish sauce, Tamarind Liquid, and/or lime juice to achieve a good balance of sweet, salty, and sour. Transfer to a serving dish, sprinkle with the lime zest, and serve warm.

Makes 4 to 6 servings.

CENDOL
Malaysian

SWEET MILK WITH JELLIES

Throughout Southeast Asia, icy glasses of milk sweetened with palm-sugar syrup are served to soothe the savage heat of the sun and the fire of chile-laden dishes. Scoops of jellied tidbits are added to the glass to create seductive combinations. My Malaysian recipe features pellets of jelly fashioned by thickening sweetened water with mung bean flour, a very fine powder from dried mung beans and sometimes available already tinted green or pink.

The center glass in the photo contains the variation made with chopped agar-agar jellies. ❧

SWEET MILK WITH JELLIES

Coconut milk is traditional, but I find drinking the gritty bits that result from chilling it unappealing and, like some Southeast Asians, prefer canned evaporated milk. Fresh milk may be substituted if you want a less rich drink. The drinks may also be prepared without any type of milk, using only palm-sugar syrup and iced water, sometimes flavored with vanilla, jasmine, or rose extract.

4 cups Fresh Coconut Milk, Thin Variation (page 141); or 2 cups canned coconut milk diluted with 2 cups fresh cow's milk or water; or 4 cups canned evaporated milk
Palm-Sugar Syrup (page 153)
3 tablespoons mung bean flour (see recipe introduction), arrowroot, or cornstarch
2 teaspoons sugar
1 cup water
Red and green food coloring
Ice cubes
Shaved or finely crushed ice

If using Fresh Coconut Milk, prepare as directed and refrigerate until chilled. If using canned milks, refrigerate to chill.

Prepare the Palm-Sugar Syrup as directed and set aside.

In a small saucepan, combine the bean flour, arrowroot, or cornstarch with the sugar and water and stir until smooth. Place over medium heat and bring to a boil, stirring constantly. Cook, stirring constantly, until the mixture is clear and quite thick, about 6 minutes. Divide the mixture evenly between 2 small bowls. Tint one with a few drops of red food coloring to create a rose-colored mixture. Tint the remaining mixture with green food coloring to create a hue that complements the rose-colored portion.

Fill a bowl with water and ice cubes and position a colander with round holes over the bowl. Pour one of the colored mixtures through the colander, using a spoon or spatula to force it through the holes into the cold water to make pellet-shaped bits. Put the remaining mixture through in the same manner. Remove the colander. When the pellets are firmly set, discard the ice and drain off the cold water.

To serve, pour about 3 tablespoons of the Palm-Sugar Syrup into the bottom of each of 4 to 6 large glasses. Add a scoop of shaved or crushed ice. Evenly distribute the jelly pellets among the glasses, then slowly pour the cold milk over them. Serve immediately.

Makes 4 to 6 servings.

VARIATION
For Vietnamese *che hot sen that tranh*, substitute chopped or shredded jelly made with agar-agar (see page 126) for the flour thickened pellets. For convenience, Asian markets stock small plastic containers of brightly colored, fruit-flavored agar-agar jellies that are ready to chop and add to drinks, as well as canned dark "grass jelly," sold by its Chinese name *leung fun*. Other alternatives or additions include cooked red or yellow mung beans, tapioca (page 125), lotus seeds, diced yam, and corn kernels.

TAPIOCA PUDDING WITH FRUIT

½ cup coconut cream scooped from the top of chilled Fresh Coconut Milk
    (page 140) or unshaken canned coconut milk
½ cup small tapioca pearls
1½ cups water
½ cup sugar
Pinch of salt
1 cup cut-up assorted fresh or canned fruits such as young coconut, jackfruit,
    longan, lychee, mango, mangosteen, palm seed, papaya, and rambutan
2 teaspoons toasted sesame seeds (optional)
Fresh mint leaves for garnish (optional)
Pesticide-free, nontoxic tropical flowers such as small orchids for garnish
    (optional)

If using Fresh Coconut Milk, prepare as directed and refrigerate until chilled. If
using canned coconut milk, reserve for later use.

Quickly rinse the tapioca under cold running water. Drain well, then transfer to a
saucepan. Add the water, sugar, and salt and stir well. Place over medium-high heat
and bring to a boil, stirring constantly, then reduce the heat so that the tapioca
barely simmers and cook, stirring frequently, until the tapioca turns translucent and
is tender when tasted, about 15 minutes. Remove from the heat.

Scoop ½ cup of the coconut cream from the top of the chilled fresh or canned
coconut milk and stir it into the warm pudding. Set aside to cool. (The remaining
coconut milk should be covered and refrigerated for another purpose.) Serve the
pudding at room temperature, or cover tightly and refrigerate until chilled.

To serve, stir the fruits into the pudding, then spoon into 4 individual dishes.
Sprinkle each serving with toasted sesame seeds (if using) and garnish with mint
and/or flowers (if using).

Makes 4 servings.

VARIATION
Burmese Tapioca Drink (*moh-let saung*). Cook the tapioca as directed, then stir in
4 cups Fresh Coconut Milk, Thin Variation (page 141), or 2 cups shaken canned
coconut milk diluted with 2 cups water. Cover tightly and chill. To serve, add a
scoop of crushed ice or small ice cubes to each of 4 glasses. Then fill each glass with
the chilled tapioca-coconut mixture, stir, and serve immediately. Offer drinking
straws and long-handled spoons.

SAKOO PAIK
Thai

TAPIOCA PUDDING WITH FRUIT

*S*outheast Asia produces most of
the world's supply of tapioca, also
known as sago, the latter of which
is the source for the Thai name for
this lightly sweetened dessert. The
pudding, with its clean, pure flavor,
is a refreshing change from the egg-
rich tapioca pudding familiar to
Westerners.

Imported tapioca comes in a mixture
of tinted hues, as well as basic white,
and varies from tiny beads to large
pearls. Actual cooking time varies
with the size of the tapioca pearls.

Any fresh or canned tropical fruit
may be added to the pudding. Cut
the fruit into bite-sized pieces before
stirring into the tapioca. ❧

AGAR-AGAR
Malaysian
KYAUK KYAW
Burmese

AGAR-AGAR PUDDING

*V*ariations on this gelatinous
pudding are common throughout
Southeast Asia wherever Chinese
settlers introduced agar-agar, an
extraction obtained from seaweed
that sets up into a very firm jelly.
It is stocked by most Asian markets,
as well as pharmacies. When using
strands or stick form, I use a postage
scale to measure the small amount
required. It may also be purchased
in a powdered form, eliminating the
need for soaking to soften. Although
agar-agar sets without refrigeration,
chilling will speed up the process.

*The clear agar-agar layer made
without coconut milk may be left
natural or tinted with food coloring.*

AGAR-AGAR PUDDING

2 cups Fresh Coconut Milk (page 140) or shaken canned coconut milk
⅓ ounce agar-agar strands or sticks, or 1 tablespoon agar-agar powder
2 cups water
6 tablespoons plus ¼ cup sugar
**5 fresh or thawed frozen screwpine (*pandan*) leaves, finely chopped; or a few
  drops *pandan* essence; or a few drops rose or jasmine extract (all optional)**
Food coloring (optional)
Fresh mint leaves for garnish (optional)

If using Fresh Coconut Milk, prepare as directed and set aside. If using canned
coconut milk, reserve for later use.

If using agar-agar strands or sticks, cut or tear into small pieces and place in a bowl.
Add cold water to cover and soak to soften for about 20 minutes. If using powdered
form, set aside for later use.

In a saucepan, combine the water, the 6 tablespoons sugar, and the screwpine
leaves (if using). Place over medium-high heat and bring to a boil. Cook, stirring
frequently, until the sugar dissolves, about 3 minutes. Remove from the heat and
set aside for 15 minutes. If using screwpine leaves, strain the liquid into a clean
saucepan.

Drain the agar-agar in a fine-mesh sieve, pressing out and discarding as much of
the water as possible, and transfer half of it to the pan containing the sugar-water
mixture, or stir ½ tablespoon of the powdered agar-agar into the mixture. Place
over medium heat and bring to a boil without stirring. Reduce the heat to low and
simmer, stirring occasionally, until the agar-agar appears completely dissolved,
8 to 10 minutes. If desired, add a few drops of *pandan* essence or rose or jasmine
extract (if using) and a few drops of green food coloring (if screwpine leaves or
essence are used) or other color (if screwpine leaves or *pandan* essence are not used)
to create an attractive shade. Strain the mixture through a fine-mesh sieve (to remove
any bits of undissolved agar-agar), dividing it equally among six 6-ounce custard
cups or molds or an 8-inch square baking dish or pan. Set aside to cool until firm,
25 to 30 minutes, or let cool slightly, then cover tightly with plastic wrap and
refrigerate until set, 15 to 20 minutes.

After the molds have set completely, pour the coconut milk into a saucepan. Add
the remaining ¼ cup of the sugar and drained or powdered agar-agar. Place over
medium heat and bring to a boil without stirring. Reduce the heat to low and
simmer, stirring occasionally, until the agar-agar appears completely dissolved, 8
to 10 minutes. Remove from the heat, strain through a fine-mesh sieve into a
pitcher, and set aside until cool but not set. Pour the coconut milk mixture evenly
over the set layer of agar-agar in each mold. Wrap tightly with plastic wrap and
refrigerate until completely set, at least 20 minutes. The mold(s) may remain
refrigerated for up to 2 days.

Recipe continues on page 128

Some Southeast Asian cooks both tint and flavor the agar-agar with the juice of tropical screwpine (pandan) leaves, thus I've given the directions. I prefer to leave it plain, however, or use a bit of rose or jasmine extract to add a subtle yet exotic flavor. ❧

To serve, dip the bottoms of the molds into hot water for a few seconds. If custard cups or molds have been used, invert the molds onto individual serving dishes. If a baking dish or pan has been used, invert the large mold onto a cutting surface and, using a sharp knife or cookie cutters, cut the pudding into diamond shapes, squares, or other designs. Garnish with mint leaves (if using).

Makes 6 servings.

RAINBOW VARIATION
Omit the coconut milk and screwpine leaves, essence, or extracts. Soften the agar-agar as directed, then drain and place in a saucepan with 4 cups water and all of the sugar. Place over medium heat and bring to a boil without stirring. Reduce the heat to low and simmer, stirring occasionally, until the agar-agar appears completely dissolved, 8 to 10 minutes. Remove from the heat and strain through a fine-mesh sieve into a pitcher. Divide the mixture among several small bowls and tint each one differently. Pour one color into the prepared molds and quickly chill to set. Top with another color and again chill to set. Repeat this until all of the colors are used, reheating each color to a pourable consistency before using.

STEAMED COCONUT CUSTARD

1 cup coconut cream scooped from the top of chilled Fresh Coconut Milk
   (page 140) or unshaken canned coconut milk
Sticky Rice (page 18)
1 cup palm sugar (see recipe introduction)
⅛ teaspoon salt
6 eggs
½ teaspoon jasmine extract (Thai *yod nam mali*; optional)
Sliced ripe mango or papaya (optional)
Pesticide-free jasmine blossoms for garnish (optional)

If using Fresh Coconut Milk, prepare as directed and refrigerate until chilled. If
using canned coconut milk, reserve for later use.

Prepare the Sticky Rice as directed. Keep warm or set aside.

To prepare for steaming, position a rack in a wok or pan that will be large enough
to hold 6 custard cups or an 8-inch round or square baking dish and can be
completely covered by a lid. Pour in water to a level just below the steaming rack
and place over high heat. Bring to a boil, then lower the heat to achieve a simmer.

Spoon 1 cup of the coconut cream from the top of the chilled fresh or canned
coconut milk into a bowl. (The remaining coconut milk should be covered and
refrigerated for another purpose.) Add the palm sugar and salt and beat or whisk
until very smooth.

In a separate bowl, crack the eggs and beat lightly with a fork until as smooth as
possible; avoid overbeating at any point to prevent too many air bubbles from
forming. Stir the eggs into the coconut cream mixture and gently blend until
smooth. Stir in the jasmine extract (if using). Strain the mixture through a fine-
mesh sieve into a pitcher. Carefully pour the mixture into six 6-ounce custard
cups or into an 8-inch round or square baking dish.

Place the custard cups or baking dish on the steamer rack. Wrap the lid of the
steamer with several layers of paper toweling or a clean kitchen towel to prevent
condensation from dripping on the top of the custard(s), then cover the steamer.
Steam until a knife inserted into the custard comes out clean, about 20 minutes
for individual custard cups, or 35 to 45 minutes for a large custard; adjust the
heat to maintain simmering water and continuous steam throughout cooking,
adding boiling water if needed to maintain water level. Remove the steamer from
the heat and uncover, being careful not to allow any condensation to drip onto
the custard(s), then transfer the custard(s) to a countertop to cool slightly.

Serve warm or at room temperature, or cover tightly and refrigerate for up to
2 days.

Recipe continues on page 131

SAHNGKAYAH
Thai

STEAMED COCONUT CUSTARD

*A*lthough it is possible to substitute
regular brown sugar or even granulated sugar in this recipe, palm
sugar is the definitive sweetener for
authentic flavor, and I urge you
to try it. Light brown palm sugar
results in a beige custard, and the
dark brown variety creates a deep
caramel color. This custard is
intensely sweet by tradition, but if
it is too sweet for your taste, the
sugar may be reduced by as much
as one-half. Keep in mind, however,
that small portions of the custard are
usually eaten as a topping on sticky
rice.

*The addition of jasmine extract (page
161) makes the custard wonderfully
exotic.*

To serve, place the custard cups on individual plates, or spoon a portion of the large custard onto each plate. (If desired, a chilled large custard can be cut into squares or diamond shapes.) Scoop portions of sticky rice alongside each serving. Add fruit slices (if using) and garnish with jasmine blossoms (if using).

Makes 6 servings.

Thai cooks often steam the custard in a hollowed-out winter squash known in America as Japanese pumpkin, kabocha, or Asian pumpkin. I've found the results to be inconsistent and the custard flavor overwhelmed by the squash. ◣

Bahn Ua Caramen
...
Vietnamese

Coconut Caramel Custard

This elegant sweet, traditional crème caramel made with Southeast Asian coconut milk and palm sugar, illustrates the influence of the long French presence in Vietnam.

Instead of individual cups, the syrup and custard can be poured into a 2-quart round baking dish, preferably metal. Bake, loosen, unmold, and garnish as directed for cups, increasing baking time to about 1 hour. ◗

COCONUT CARAMEL CUSTARD

3 cups Fresh Coconut Milk (page 140) or shaken canned coconut milk
1 cup granulated sugar
¼ cup water
3 whole eggs
5 egg yolks
½ cup palm sugar, preferably pale beige type
1 teaspoon pure vanilla extract
Pesticide-free, nontoxic tropical flowers such as small orchids for garnish (optional)

If using Fresh Coconut Milk, prepare as directed and set aside. If using canned coconut milk, reserve for later use.

Preheat an oven to 350° F.

In a heavy saucepan, combine the granulated sugar and water and stir well. Place over medium heat, cover, and heat for about 4 minutes. Remove the cover and continue to cook, swirling the pan, until the syrup turns amber, about 8 minutes longer. If sugar crystals begin to form around the sides of the pan just above the bubbling syrup, brush them away with a wet brush. Carefully pour the hot syrup into eight 6-ounce ovenproof custard cups and quickly swirl the cups to coat the bottoms and about one third of the way up the sides. Set the cups aside to cool.

In a large mixing bowl, combine the whole eggs and egg yolks and beat lightly with a fork until as smooth as possible; avoid overbeating at any point to prevent too many air bubbles from forming. Stir in the palm sugar, coconut milk, and vanilla. Slowly strain the mixture through a fine-mesh sieve into a pitcher. Carefully pour the mixture into the sugar-lined cups. Place the cups in a large baking pan, cover the cups with aluminum foil or parchment paper, and place in the oven. Pour enough hot (not boiling) water into the pan to reach about two thirds of the way up the sides of the cups.

Bake until a knife inserted near the edge of the custard comes out barely clean, about 35 minutes; the center should still wobble slightly when a cup is shaken. Regulate the oven temperature during baking to maintain water at the almost simmering stage; do not allow to boil. Remove from the hot water to a countertop, remove the foil or paper, and let cool slightly.

To serve warm, run a thin, sharp knife around the inside of each cup to loosen the custard. Cover with an inverted individual serving plate and invert the custard. Lift off the cup; caramel syrup will run down onto the serving dish to surround the custard. Garnish with flowers (if using).

To serve cold, let cool to room temperature, then cover tightly and refrigerate until well chilled, at least 3 hours or as long as overnight. Just before serving, immerse the bottom of each cup in a pan of hot water for about 30 seconds, then loosen custard, unmold, and garnish as above.

Makes 8 servings.

FROZEN COCONUT CREAM

4 cups Fresh Coconut Milk (page 140) or shaken canned coconut milk
1½ cups Simple Sugar Syrup (page 153), or to taste
Toasted fresh or dried shredded coconut or chopped unsalted dry-roasted
    peanuts (optional)

If using Fresh Coconut Milk, prepare as directed and set aside. If using canned coconut milk, reserve for later use.

Prepare the Simple Sugar Syrup as directed.

In a bowl, combine the coconut milk and syrup and blend well. Cover tightly and refrigerate until well chilled, at least 3 hours or, preferably, overnight.

Just before freezing, whisk or stir the chilled coconut mixture as smoothly as possible. Pour into an ice cream maker and freeze according to the manufacturer's instructions until the mixture is frozen yet still soft.

Scoop into 4 serving dishes, sprinkle with the coconut or peanuts (if using), and serve immediately. Alternatively, pack into a container with a tight-fitting lid and place in a freezer for several hours; transfer to the refrigerator about 20 minutes before serving, to allow it to reach the proper consistency.

Makes 4 servings.

VARIATION
Stir ½ cup cooked fresh corn kernels and/or 1 cup shredded young coconut meat into the chilled custard just before freezing.

IDEM GA-TI
Thai

FROZEN COCONUT CREAM

Wonderful with Fried Bananas (page 136), this softly frozen sweet, a cross between sorbet and ice cream, is one time when freshly made coconut milk is preferable to canned. Don't expect a firm American-style ice cream; the results are more akin to a soft Italian gelato.

135

Although I find the smooth texture in my recipe more appealing, cooked corn kernels and shredded young coconut are traditional additions. Fresh young coconut, with a fairly soft beige husk instead of the familiar hairy brown shell, is sometimes available in natural-foods stores or Asian markets, where the shredded meat may also be available frozen. ❧

GLUAY TORD
...
Thai

PISANG GORENG
...
Indonesian and Malaysian

FRIED BANANAS

Choose bananas that have just turned yellow all over; overripe ones will fall apart during frying. If desired, roll the batter-coated bananas in shredded sweetened dried coconut and/or sesame seeds before frying, or sprinkle the fried bananas with toasted shredded coconut and/or sesame seeds after frying. Dusting the fried fruit with ground cardamom and powdered sugar adds a flavorful and festive touch.

Don't overlook the tantalizing fried pineapple variation. ❧

FRIED BANANAS

For a special treat, serve with Frozen Coconut Cream (page 135) or a favorite vanilla, coconut, or ginger ice cream, or top with dollops of coconut cream sweetened to taste with palm sugar.

⅔ cup Fresh Coconut Milk (page 140) or shaken canned coconut milk
½ cup all-purpose flour
½ cup rice flour
1 tablespoon sugar
1 teaspoon baking powder
¼ teaspoon salt
2 eggs
Canola oil or other high-quality vegetable oil for deep-frying
6 large, ripe but firm bananas, or 12 finger-sized bananas

If using Fresh Coconut Milk, prepare as directed and set aside. If using canned coconut milk, reserve for later use.

In a bowl, combine the flours, sugar, baking powder, and salt and mix well. In a separate bowl, lightly beat the eggs, then stir in the coconut milk until well blended. Stir into the flour mixture and beat with a wire whisk or wooden spoon until smooth. Cover and refrigerate for about 2 hours.

In a wok, deep-fat fryer, or large, deep pan such as a dutch oven, pour in oil to a depth of 2 inches. Heat to 375° F, or until a small piece of bread dropped into the hot oil turns golden brown within about 30 seconds. Place a wire rack over a baking sheet; set aside.

While the oil is heating, peel the bananas. Slice each large one crosswise into 3 pieces of equal length; leave small bananas whole.

Dip a piece of banana in the batter to coat completely and carefully lower into the hot oil. Add only a few pieces at a time to avoid crowding the pan. Fry, turning several times, until golden brown all over, about 3 minutes. Using a slotted utensil, transfer the bananas to the wire rack to drain briefly. Cook the remaining bananas in the same way, allowing the oil to return to 375° F between batches.

Arrange on a platter or individual plates and serve warm.

Makes 6 servings.

VARIATION
Fried Pineapple (Thai *sapbhalot tord* or Indonesian and Malaysian *nanas goreng*). For the bananas, substitute 6 round, fresh pineapple slices, each about ½ inch thick and cut into 3 wedges. Pat dry with paper toweling before dipping into the batter.

SARNWIN MAKIN
· · ·
Burmese

SEMOLINA CAKE

I encountered this dense sweet at San Francisco's Mandalay restaurant, where it is billed as sui gi mok *and charmingly described as topped with "puppy seed." It has been "puppy seed cake" around my house ever since, though I also enjoy it topped with sesame seeds.*

This recipe reflects the Indian influence on the cooking of old Burma. Many versions call for ghee, *clarified butter with no trace of milk solids; if you have access to* ghee, *or wish to make your own, use it in place of the butter. Many supermarkets now stock semolina for use in making Italian pasta, but I find that readily available Cream of Wheat works just as well.* ❧

SEMOLINA CAKE

3 cups Fresh Coconut Milk (page 140) or shaken canned coconut milk
1 cup fine semolina flour or Cream of Wheat (not instant)
⅔ cup palm sugar
½ teaspoon ground cardamom
⅛ teaspoon salt
4 tablespoons (½ stick) unsalted butter
3 eggs
3 to 4 tablespoons poppy seeds, preferably white variety, or sesame seeds
¼ cup (½ stick) unsalted butter, melted, for drizzling

If using Fresh Coconut Milk, prepare as directed and set aside. If using canned coconut milk, reserve for later use.

Heat a sauté pan or heavy skillet over medium heat. Add the semolina or Cream of Wheat and heat, stirring constantly, until toasted, about 10 minutes. Remove from the heat and set aside.

Preheat an oven to 300° F. Lightly grease an 8- or 9-inch square baking pan; set aside.

In a heavy saucepan, combine the coconut milk, sugar, cardamom, and salt and beat or whisk until smooth. Gradually beat or whisk in the toasted semolina or Cream of Wheat until the mixture is very smooth. Place over medium heat and cook, stirring or whisking to prevent lumps, until it begins to thicken, about 5 minutes. Stir in the 4 tablespoons butter, 1 tablespoon at a time, until it melts. Continue cooking, stirring constantly, until the mixture is very thick and pulls away from the sides of the pan, about 5 minutes longer. Remove from the heat and let cool slightly.

In a bowl, lightly beat the eggs. Beat or whisk about ½ cup of the warm semolina mixture into the eggs, then transfer the eggs to the pan of warm semolina and beat or whisk until smooth. Spread the mixture in the prepared baking dish, smoothing the top with the back of a wooden spoon. Sprinkle the poppy or sesame seeds evenly over the surface, then drizzle the melted butter evenly over the top.

Bake until the surface of the cake is lightly browned and the interior is firmly set when the top is touched in the center, about 45 minutes. Transfer to a wire rack and let cool completely.

Cut into diamond-shaped pieces about 2 inches wide by 3 inches long or into 2-inch squares and serve at room temperature. Servings may be briefly reheated in a microwave oven and served warm.

Makes 8 servings.

GA-TI
Thai

NUOC COT DUA
Vietnamese

SANTAN
Indonesian and Malaysian

FRESH COCONUT MILK

Traditionally, coconut milk is made by steeping grated coconut in hot water. The extracted results are known as thick, or regular, coconut milk. For thinner versions, see the variations after the recipe. A richer coconut milk can be achieved by using hot milk in place of the water.

Whether freshly made or canned, when coconut milk is cooled, a thick oily layer of "cream" rises to the top. It may be used in place of oil in cooking or stirred into dishes to add richness, or it may be blended into the coconut milk much like cream is homogenized into whole cow's milk.

140

BASICS

The following recipes, beginning with the directions for making fresh coconut milk, are essential elements of Southeast Asian cooking. Many basics, such as the Thai curry pastes and the Indonesian chile sauces, can be made ahead and stored in the refrigerator for weeks, ready to use when you feel the urge to create a delectable Southeast Asian dish.

Southeast Asian kitchens and tables rely heavily on dipping sauces and condiments, which cooks and diners traditionally use to adjust the flavors and the degree of heat of their dishes. You may also discover that many of these Southeast Asian pantry staples can add a welcome zest to your Western dishes, such as salad dressings, soups, stews, burgers, grilled meats, and vegetables. Home-pickled garlic and ginger, for example, have become indispensible items in my kitchen for a wide range of uses.

FRESH COCONUT MILK

1 mature coconut, or 4 cups shredded or flaked unsweetened dried coconut (sold as "desiccated coconut" in natural-foods stores) or thawed frozen grated coconut
2 cups boiling water

If using a whole coconut, preheat an oven to 400° F. If using shredded, flaked, or grated coconut, skip the next three paragraphs.

Using an ice pick or a nail, pierce holes in the three indented "eyes" on the top of the whole coconut, invert, and drain out the clear juice into a container. Taste the juice to be sure it is sweet; if rancid, discard and start with a fresh coconut. If the juice is good, drink it as a cook's treat or include it as part of the boiling water used to make the coconut milk.

Place the coconut in the oven for 15 minutes, which usually cracks the shell and will cause the pulp to pull away from the shell for easier removal. Transfer to a countertop. If the shell did not crack from the heat, hold it with one hand and hit it with a hammer or the blunt edge of a heavy cleaver until the shell cracks. Using an oyster knife or other similar instrument, pry the shell open. With the oyster knife or a dull table knife, pry out sections of the white pulp from the shell.

Using a small, sharp knife or a vegetable peeler, remove the brown skin from the white pulp. Rinse the pulp under cold running water to remove any brown fiber that has clung from the shell. Using a hand grater or food processor, finely grate or chop the coconut; there should be about 4 cups.

Place the coconut in a bowl, pour the boiling water over it, stir to mix well, and let steep for 30 minutes. Working in batches, if necessary, transfer the coconut and liquid to a blender or food processor fitted with a steel blade and blend until the mixture is as smooth as possible.

Line a fine-mesh sieve with several layers of dampened cheesecloth and set over a clean bowl. Strain the coconut mixture through the sieve, pushing against the strainer with a wooden spoon, then wrap the cheesecloth around the coconut pulp and squeeze to extract as much liquid as possible. Use immediately, or cover tightly and refrigerate for up to 2 days; the milk must be chilled in order for the coconut cream to rise to the top. Do not freeze, as the velvety texture will be destroyed.

When a recipe calls for coconut cream, scoop off and use the thick layer that rises to the top of the chilled liquid. When coconut milk is called for, stir the thick cream and the thin liquid underneath together until smooth before using.

Makes about 2 cups.

VARIATIONS
Medium Coconut Milk. Prepare regular coconut milk as in basic recipe and set aside. Cover the same drained coconut pulp with 2 cups boiling water and repeat the process. Combine the two batches of coconut milk. Makes about 4 cups.

Thin Coconut Milk. Prepare regular coconut milk as in basic recipe and use for another purpose. Cover the same drained coconut pulp with 2 cups boiling water and repeat the process. Use the second batch for recipes calling for thin coconut milk. Makes about 2 cups regular and 2 cups thin.

USING CANNED COCONUT MILK
When using canned coconut milk, always read the recipe prior to disturbing or opening the can to know whether it should be shaken first.

Coconut Cream. Open canned coconut milk without shaking it and scoop off the thick layer of coconut cream.

Regular or Thick Coconut Milk. Shake canned coconut milk to blend well before opening the can.

Medium Coconut Milk. Shake canned coconut milk to blend well before opening the can, then dilute with half a can of water.

Thin Coconut Milk. Shake canned coconut milk to blend well before opening the can, then dilute with an equal amount of water.

Although the recipe will teach you how to make coconut milk, the process is time-consuming, so for most dishes I reach for unsweetened canned coconut milk, imported from Southeast Asia (see Shopping Guide on page 160).

Some recipes call for a specific type of coconut milk, which may be obtained by following directions in the recipe variations or by using canned milk as directed.

Traditional coconut graters, sometimes available in stores that sell Southeast Asian foods, can be used to grate coconut pulp directly from a cracked shell. ❧

141

RED CURRY PASTE

KRUENG GAENG PEHT
Thai

RED CURRY PASTE

This essential ingredient of many Thai dishes gets its color and fire from the addition of dried red chilies. It is generally paired with beef, pork, and fish, but can be used with any meat, fish, or poultry.

Although toasted whole spice seeds yield more flavor, ground spices may be substituted for the whole.

Even when mixing curry pastes in a food processor, the ingredients should be coarsely chopped for measuring and easier blending.

All curry pastes keep well for several weeks in the refrigerator. They should be stored in glass containers; plastic storage containers become too permeated with the intense fragrance to reuse for other purposes. ❧

142

½ cup small dried red hot chiles, preferably Thai bird variety
¼ teaspoon black peppercorns
1 tablespoon coriander seeds
1 teaspoon cumin seeds
3 tablespoons chopped fresh lemongrass, tender bulb portion only
3 tablespoons coarsely chopped garlic
¼ cup coarsely chopped shallot
1 tablespoon coarsely chopped fresh galanga or ginger
1 tablespoon coarsely chopped fresh cilantro, preferably from root or lower stem portions
2 teaspoons minced fresh lime zest
1 teaspoon bottled moist shrimp paste (Thai *ga-pi*)
1 teaspoon salt

Discard the stems from the chiles and shake out the seeds if desired. Place in a small bowl, add warm water to cover, and let stand until softened, about 20 minutes.

In a small skillet, combine the peppercorns and the coriander and cumin seeds. Place over medium heat and toast, stirring or shaking the pan frequently, until fragrant, 3 to 5 minutes; do not allow to burn. Pour onto a plate to cool, then transfer to a spice grinder or heavy mortar with a pestle and grind to a fine powder. Set aside.

Drain the chiles, reserving the soaking water, and transfer to a food processor, blender, or heavy mortar with a pestle. Add the lemongrass, garlic, shallot, galanga or ginger, cilantro, and lime zest and chop or pound until well mixed. Add the shrimp paste, salt, and the ground toasted spices. Blend to a thick paste, adding up to 3 tablespoons of the chile soaking water if needed to facilitate blending.

Use immediately, or transfer to a small glass jar, cover tightly, and refrigerate for up to 4 weeks.

Makes about ⅔ cup.

GREEN CURRY PASTE

1 teaspoon black or white peppercorns
4 whole cloves
2 teaspoons coriander seeds
1 teaspoon cumin seeds
1 teaspoon fennel seeds
3 tablespoons chopped fresh lemongrass, tender bulb portion only
3 tablespoons coarsely chopped fresh galanga or ginger
3 tablespoons chopped fresh green hot chile, preferably Thai bird variety,
  seeded if desired
3 tablespoons coarsely chopped shallot
2 tablespoons coarsely chopped garlic
2 teaspoons freshly grated lime zest
1 teaspoon bottled moist shrimp paste (Thai *ga-pi*)
1 teaspoon salt
½ cup chopped fresh cilantro (coriander), including roots, stems, and leaves
Canola oil or other high-quality vegetable oil for storing (optional)

In a small skillet, combine the peppercorns, cloves, and the coriander, cumin, and fennel seeds. Place over medium heat and toast, stirring or shaking the pan frequently, until fragrant, 3 to 5 minutes; do not allow to burn. Pour onto a plate to cool, then transfer to a spice grinder or heavy mortar with a pestle and grind to a fine powder. Set aside.

In a food processor, blender, or heavy mortar with a pestle, combine the lemongrass, galanga or ginger, chile, shallot, garlic, and lime zest and chop or pound until well mixed. Add the shrimp paste, salt, cilantro, and the ground toasted spices. Blend to a thick paste, adding up to 3 tablespoons water if needed to facilitate blending.

Use immediately, or transfer to a small glass jar, top with a thin layer of oil to prevent air from darkening the paste, cover tightly, and refrigerate for up to 4 weeks.

Makes about 1 cup.

---

*KRUENG GAENG KIOW
WAHN*
...
Thai

GREEN CURRY PASTE

Green curries are favored by Thai cooks for chicken, fish, and vegetables, as well as for special religious feasts.

A thin layer of oil over the top of the paste helps preserve the bright green color of the chiles and cilantro.

143

Please read the introduction to Red Curry Paste (page 142) for general information on making and storing curry pastes. ❧

YELLOW CURRY PASTE

*M*ilder than Thai green or red curry pastes, this version is more closely akin to the familiar golden curry powders of India. Thai cooks combine it with chicken, fish, and shellfish.

Please read the introduction to Red Curry Paste (page 142) for general information on making and storing curry pastes. ❧

144

3 tablespoons small dried red hot chiles, preferably Thai bird variety
2 tablespoons coriander seeds
2 tablespoons cumin seeds
3 tablespoons chopped fresh lemongrass, tender bulb portion only
3 tablespoons coarsely chopped fresh galanga or ginger
¼ cup coarsely chopped shallot
3 tablespoons coarsely chopped garlic
1 teaspoon bottled moist shrimp paste (Thai *ga-pi*)
2 teaspoons salt
2 teaspoons ground turmeric

Discard the stems from the chiles and shake out the seeds if desired. Place in a small bowl, add warm water to cover, and let stand until softened, about 20 minutes.

In a small skillet, combine the coriander and cumin seeds. Place over medium heat and toast, stirring or shaking the pan frequently, until fragrant, 3 to 5 minutes; do not allow to burn. Pour onto a plate to cool, then transfer to a spice grinder or heavy mortar with a pestle and grind to a fine powder. Set aside.

Drain the chiles, reserving the soaking water, and transfer to a food processor, blender, or heavy mortar with a pestle. Add the lemongrass, galanga or ginger, shallot, and garlic and chop or pound until well mixed. Add the shrimp paste, salt, turmeric, and the ground toasted spices. Blend to a thick paste, adding up to 3 tablespoons of the chile soaking water if needed to facilitate blending.

Use immediately, or transfer to a small glass jar, cover tightly, and refrigerate for up to 4 weeks.

Makes about 1 cup.

MUSSAMUN CURRY PASTE

2 tablespoons small dried red hot chiles, preferably Thai bird variety
1½ tablespoons cumin seeds
½ teaspoon coriander seeds
½ teaspoon cardamom seeds
½ teaspoon black or white peppercorns
½ teaspoon cloves
2 tablespoons chopped lemongrass, tender bulb portion only
1 tablespoon coarsely chopped fresh galanga or ginger
⅓ cup coarsely chopped shallot
¼ cup coarsely chopped garlic
1½ teaspoons bottled moist shrimp paste (Thai *ga-pi*)
1 teaspoon salt
1 teaspoon freshly grated nutmeg
½ teaspoon ground cinnamon

Discard the stems from the chiles and shake out the seeds if desired. Place in a small bowl, add warm water to cover, and let stand until softened, about 20 minutes.

In a small skillet, combine the cumin, coriander, and cardamom seeds, peppercorns, and cloves. Place over medium heat and toast, stirring or shaking the pan frequently, until fragrant, 3 to 5 minutes; do not allow to burn. Pour onto a plate to cool, then transfer to a spice grinder or heavy mortar with a pestle and grind to a fine powder. Set aside.

Drain the chiles, reserving the soaking water, and transfer to a food processor, blender, or heavy mortar with a pestle. Add the lemongrass, galanga or ginger, shallot, and garlic and chop or pound until well mixed. Add the shrimp paste, salt, nutmeg, cinnamon, and the ground toasted spices. Blend to a thick paste, adding up to 3 tablespoons of the chile soaking water if needed to facilitate blending.

Use immediately, or transfer to a small glass jar, cover tightly, and refrigerate for up to 4 weeks.

Makes about ¾ cup.

BASICS

*KRUNENG GAENG
MUSSAMUN*
· · ·
Thai

MUSSAMUN CURRY PASTE

*I*ndian immigrants introduced their spices to Thailand, where they were incorporated into various recipes, including this paste, which is customarily teamed with beef to make exotically flavored curries.

Please read the introduction to Red Curry Paste (page 142) for general information on making and storing curry pastes. ◥

145

NAHN JEEM GRATIEM
Thai

SWEET CHILE-GARLIC DIPPING SAUCE

This sauce is a traditional accompaniment to Thai-style barbecued chicken. It also pairs well with spring rolls and any fried or grilled food. ❧

NAM MAKAHM
Thai
NUOC CHAM ME
Vietnamese

TAMARIND DIPPING SAUCE

Here is a tasty addition to fried or grilled fish or cooked vegetables such as Stuffed Eggplant (page 65). ❧

146

SWEET CHILE-GARLIC DIPPING SAUCE

2 cups distilled white vinegar
1 cup sugar
4 teaspoons salt
4 teaspoons bottled chile-garlic sauce (Vietnamese *tuong ot toi*), or 2 teaspoons minced garlic and 2 teaspoons crushed dried red chile flakes

In a small saucepan, combine all the ingredients and bring to a boil over medium heat. Cook, stirring occasionally, until the mixture is syrupy and reduced to slightly more than 1 cup, about 30 minutes. (The sauce will thicken further as it cools.)

Serve warm or at room temperature, or cover tightly and refrigerate indefinitely.

Makes about 1 cup.

TAMARIND DIPPING SAUCE

½ cup Tamarind Liquid (page 156), or to taste
1 tablespoon Red Curry Paste (page 142) or canned Thai red curry paste, or to taste
2 tablespoons canola oil or other high-quality vegetable oil
3 tablespoons minced or pressed garlic
2 tablespoons minced fresh ginger
¼ cup fish sauce
¼ cup soy sauce
¼ cup palm sugar
2 tablespoons minced fresh cilantro (coriander)
2 tablespoons minced fresh green onion, including green tops

Prepare the Tamarind Liquid and set aside.

If using Red Curry Paste, prepare as directed and set aside. If using canned curry paste, reserve for later use.

In a small saucepan, heat the oil over medium heat. Add the curry paste and cook, stirring constantly, until fragrant, about 1 minute. Add the garlic and ginger and cook about 1 minute longer. Stir in the Tamarind Liquid, fish sauce, soy sauce, and sugar. Stir until the sugar dissolves. Stir in the cilantro and green onion, reduce the heat to low, and simmer until the sauce is slightly thickened, about 2 minutes longer. Taste and adjust the amount of tamarind, fish sauce, and sugar to create a good balance of sour, salty, and sweet.

Serve warm or at room temperature, or cover tightly and refrigerate for up to 2 days.

Makes about 1 cup.

CHILE DIPPING SAUCE, THAI STYLE

Softened dried shrimp, tiny round eggplants, minced onion, Asian sesame oil, and other ingredients may be added to taste to the basic sauce.

¼ cup minced or sliced fresh green or red hot chile
2 teaspoons minced or pressed garlic (optional)
¼ cup freshly squeezed lime juice or distilled white vinegar
3 tablespoons fish sauce

In a bowl, combine all of the ingredients and mix well.

Serve at room temperature, or cover tightly and refrigerate for up to 2 months.

Makes about ¾ cup.

CHILE DIPPING SAUCE, VIETNAMESE STYLE

2 tablespoons coarsely chopped garlic
2 tablespoons coarsely chopped fresh red hot chile, or to taste
½ cup fish sauce
3 tablespoons sugar, or to taste
¼ cup distilled white vinegar
¼ cup freshly squeezed lime juice
½ cup water
2 tablespoons finely chopped unsalted dry-roasted peanuts (optional)
2 tablespoons finely shredded or grated carrot (optional)

In a food processor or blender, combine the garlic, chile, fish sauce, sugar, vinegar, lime juice, and water and blend well. Alternatively, in a heavy mortar with a pestle, combine the garlic, chile, and 1 tablespoon of the fish sauce and blend to a paste. Add the remaining fish sauce, sugar, vinegar, lime juice, and water and blend to dissolve the sugar.

Serve at room temperature, or cover tightly and refrigerate for up to 2 months. Just before serving, stir in the peanuts and carrot (if using).

Makes about 1½ cups.

147

BASICS

NAM PRIK
Thai

CHILE DIPPING SAUCE, THAI STYLE

*N*early all Thai cooks make a version of this sauce, which appears with nearly every meal and is used along with crushed dried red chiles and chopped peanuts for seasoning dishes. ❧

NUOC CHAM
Vietnamese

CHILE DIPPING SAUCE, VIETNAMESE STYLE

*N*umerous variations exist for this ubiquitous condiment that is used for dipping spring rolls and seasoning many other dishes in Vietnam, much as salt and pepper are used on the American table. To save time, substitute ¼ cup chile-garlic sauce (Vietnamese tuong ot toi) for the fresh garlic and chile. ❧

NAM PRIK PLA
Thai

SPICY FISH DIPPING SAUCE

*A*n all-purpose table sauce that is great with fried fish. ◗

148

SAMBAL ULEK
Indonesian

RED CHILE SAUCE

*B*oth the salt and vinegar help preserve the flavor and color of the fresh chiles. The sauce is available in Asian markets, but a homemade batch tastes fresher. It is used both in cooking and as a table condiment. ◗

SPICY FISH DIPPING SAUCE

⅓ cup fish sauce
⅓ cup water
¼ cup palm sugar
¼ cup freshly squeezed lime juice or distilled white vinegar
2 tablespoons minced Pickled Garlic (page 155), or 2 teaspoons minced fresh garlic
1 tablespoon minced fresh red hot chile, or 1 teaspoon ground dried red hot chile, or to taste
3 tablespoons peeled, seeded, and chopped cucumber (optional)
¼ cup finely chopped or ground unsalted dry-roasted peanuts

In a small saucepan, combine the fish sauce, water, and sugar. Place over medium heat and bring to a boil. Cook, stirring frequently, until the sugar dissolves and the mixture is reduced to the consistency of a thin syrup, about 5 minutes. Remove from the heat and transfer to a bowl. Add the lime juice or vinegar, garlic, and chile and mix well.

Serve at room temperature, or cover tightly and refrigerate for up to 3 weeks. Just before serving, stir in the cucumber (if using) and peanuts.

Makes about 1 cup.

RED CHILE SAUCE

1 teaspoon Tamarind Liquid (page 156) or distilled white vinegar
1 cup coarsely chopped fresh red hot chile, including seeds
1 teaspoon salt

If using Tamarind Liquid, prepare as directed. If using vinegar, reserve.

In a food processor, blender, or heavy mortar with a pestle, combine the chile with the salt and Tamarind Liquid or vinegar. Blend to a thick paste.

Serve at room temperature, or cover tightly and refrigerate for up to 3 days if made with Tamarind Liquid or up to 1 month if made with vinegar.

Makes about ½ cup.

DRIED CHILE VARIATION
Cut off and discard stems from 1 cup small dried red hot chiles. Using kitchen shears, cut chiles into small pieces into a saucepan. Add enough water to cover barely. Place over medium heat and bring to a boil. Reduce the heat to maintain a simmer and cook the chiles until soft, about 5 minutes. Drain well, then transfer to a mini food processor, blender, or heavy mortar with a pestle. Add the Tamarind Liquid or vinegar and salt and blend to a paste.

COOKED RED CHILE SAUCE

¼ cup Tamarind Liquid (page 156) or distilled white vinegar
1 cup coarsely chopped fresh red hot chile, including seeds
1 cup coarsely chopped shallot
2 tablespoons coarsely chopped garlic
3 tablespoons coarsely chopped candlenuts
1 slice firm dried shrimp paste (Indonesian *trasi* or Malaysian *blachan*),
    about ½ inch thick and ¾ inch square, crumbled
3 tablespoons canola oil or other high-quality vegetable oil
4 teaspoons palm sugar
About 1 teaspoon salt

If using Tamarind Liquid, prepare as directed and set aside. If using vinegar, reserve for later use.

In a food processor, blender, or heavy mortar with a pestle, combine the chile, shallot, garlic, nuts, and shrimp paste and blend to a thick paste, adding about 1 tablespoon of water if needed to facilitate blending.

In a small skillet, heat the oil over medium heat. Add the chile mixture and cook, stirring constantly, until fragrant, 2 to 3 minutes. Stir in the Tamarind Liquid or vinegar, sugar, and salt to taste. Simmer until the liquid has evaporated and the oil begins to separate from the paste, about 8 minutes. Remove from the heat and let cool to room temperature.

Serve at room temperature, or cover tightly and refrigerate for up to 3 days if using Tamarind Liquid or up to 1 month if using vinegar.

Makes about 1 cup.

SWEET SOY SAUCE

½ cup soy sauce
1 cup palm sugar

In a small saucepan, combine the ingredients. Place over medium heat and bring to a boil. Cook, stirring frequently, until the mixture is syrupy, about 5 minutes. (The sauce will thicken further as it cools.) Remove from the heat and let cool to room temperature.

Use immediately, or cover tightly and store at room temperature for up to 2 weeks.

Makes about 1 cup.

SAMBAL BAJAK
• • •
Indonesian

COOKED RED CHILE SAUCE

*C*hoose small red hot chiles such as Thai bird or California serrano. The heat will vary according to the chiles. ❧

KECAP MANIS
• • •
Indonesian
KECHAP
• • •
Malaysian
SI-YU WAHN
• • •
Thai

149

SWEET SOY SAUCE

*T*his dark, thick sauce is a staple condiment of the Indonesian kitchen and table. Its Malaysian name, which refers to a variety of preserved sauces made from either soybean or fish, was borrowed for Western-style catsup.

In Thailand and in Chinese communities throughout Southeast Asia, sweet soy sauce adds rich color and flavor to a variety of dishes. ❧

NAM JIM
Thai

PEANUT SAUCE, THAI STYLE

*T*he Thais prefer a peanut sauce
with a balance of sweet, sour, spicy,
and salty tastes. ❧

150

1 cup coconut cream scooped from the top of chilled Fresh Coconut Milk
   (page 140) or unshaken canned coconut milk
¼ cup Red Curry Paste (page 142) or canned Thai red curry paste, or to taste
¼ cup Tamarind Liquid (page 156)
1 cup unsalted dry-roasted peanuts, or 1 cup smooth peanut butter
2 tablespoons peanut oil or other high-quality vegetable oil, if using whole
   peanuts
1 cup homemade chicken stock or canned reduced-sodium chicken broth
6 tablespoons palm sugar
2 tablespoons fish sauce
About 1 teaspoon salt

If using Fresh Coconut Milk, prepare as directed and refrigerate until chilled. If
using canned coconut milk, reserve for later use.

If using Red Curry Paste, prepare as directed and set aside. If using canned curry
paste, reserve for later use.

Prepare Tamarind Liquid as directed and set aside.

If using peanuts, in a blender or food processor, combine the peanuts and the oil
and blend until a fairly smooth butter forms; set aside. If using prepared peanut
butter, reserve for later use.

Scoop 1 cup of the coconut cream from the top of the chilled fresh or canned
coconut milk and transfer to a small saucepan. (The remaining coconut milk should
be covered and refrigerated for another use.) Place over medium heat and bring to a
boil. Stir in the curry paste and cook, stirring constantly, until quite fragrant, about
5 minutes. Stir in the peanut butter, stock or broth, and sugar. Reduce the heat to
maintain a simmer and cook, stirring frequently, until the sauce is smooth and
thickened, about 5 minutes. Remove from the heat and stir in the Tamarind Liquid,
fish sauce, and salt to taste. Pour into a bowl.

Serve warm or at room temperature, or cover tightly and refrigerate for up to 5
days. If the sauce becomes too thick during storage, thin with coconut milk or
slowly reheat just before serving to achieve a consistency for dipping.

Makes about 2 cups.

PEANUT SAUCE, INDONESIAN STYLE

1¾ cups Fresh Coconut Milk (page 140) or shaken canned coconut milk
⅔ cup unsalted dry-roasted peanuts, or ⅔ cup smooth peanut butter
1 or 3 tablespoons peanut oil or other high-quality vegetable oil
2 teaspoons minced or pressed garlic
1 teaspoon grated fresh ginger
¼ cup homemade chicken stock or canned reduced-sodium chicken broth
3 tablespoons soy sauce
2 tablespoons palm sugar
Salt
Ground cayenne pepper
¼ cup freshly squeezed lime juice

If using Fresh Coconut Milk, prepare as directed and set aside. If using canned coconut milk, reserve for later use.

If using peanuts, in a blender or food processor, combine the peanuts and 2 tablespoons of the oil and blend until a fairly smooth butter forms; set aside. If using prepared peanut butter, reserve.

In a small saucepan, heat 1 tablespoon oil over medium heat. Add the garlic and ginger and cook, stirring constantly, until the garlic just begins to change color; do not brown. Stir in the peanut butter, coconut milk, stock or broth, soy sauce, sugar, and salt and cayenne pepper to taste. Bring to a boil, then adjust the heat to maintain a simmer and cook, stirring frequently, until the sauce is smooth and thickened, about 5 minutes. Remove from the heat and stir in the lime juice. Pour into a bowl.

Serve warm or at room temperature, or cover tightly and refrigerate for up to 5 days. If the sauce becomes too thick during storage, thin with coconut milk or slowly reheat just before serving to achieve a consistency for dipping.

Makes about 2 cups.

SAUS KACHANG TANAH
• • •
Indonesian and Malaysian

PEANUT SAUCE, INDONESIAN STYLE

*S*mooth and creamy, this sauce makes a great foil for sate and other spicy fare. ❧

PEANUT SAUCE, VIETNAMESE STYLE

PEANUT SAUCE, VIETNAMESE STYLE

Ground pork is sometimes added to Vietnamese peanut sauce, although I prefer this lighter version as a dipping sauce. If you can locate Vietnamese bean sauce (tuong) made from soybeans and roasted glutinous rice, substitute about ¼ cup for the cooked glutinous rice and Chinese bean sauce. ❧

152

1 teaspoon Red Chile Sauce (page 148) or bottled red chile sauce (Vietnamese *tuong ot* or Indonesian *sambal ulek*)
¼ cup glutinous rice
1½ cups water
1 teaspoon canola oil or other high-quality vegetable oil
1 teaspoon minced garlic
1 cup homemade chicken stock or canned reduced-sodium chicken broth
2 tablespoons Chinese brown or yellow bean sauce (*jiang*)
1 tablespoon sugar
2 teaspoons fish sauce
½ cup finely ground unsalted dry-roasted peanuts or smooth peanut butter

If using Red Chile Sauce, prepare as directed and set aside. If using bottled chile sauce, reserve for later use.

In a saucepan, combine the rice and water. Bring to a boil over high heat, then cover, reduce the heat to low, and simmer until the rice is very soft and the water is absorbed, about 45 minutes. Remove from the heat and set aside.

In another saucepan, heat the oil over medium-low heat. Add the garlic and cook, stirring constantly, until it just begins to change color, about 1 minute; do not brown. Stir in the stock or broth, bean sauce, sugar, fish sauce, and the cooked rice. Increase the heat to bring the mixture to a simmer, then adjust the heat to maintain a simmer and cook, stirring frequently, until the sauce is thickened, about 5 minutes. Remove from the heat and stir in the ground peanuts or peanut butter and chile sauce. Pour into a bowl.

Serve warm or at room temperature, or cover tightly and refrigerate for up to 5 days. If the sauce becomes too thick during storage, thin with water or slowly reheat just before serving to achieve a consistency for dipping.

Makes about 2½ cups.

VARIATION
For a heartier sauce, add 4 ounces ground pork along with the garlic and stir-fry until just past the pink stage, about 2 minutes. Then proceed as directed.

GINGER SYRUP

2 quarts water
1 pound fresh ginger, coarsely chopped
4 cups sugar

In a large saucepan over high heat, bring the water and ginger to a boil. Reduce the heat to medium and simmer, uncovered, for 1 hour. Remove from the heat, let cool slightly, and then strain the liquid.

Measure the ginger-flavored liquid and add enough hot water if necessary to equal 4 cups. Place the liquid in a clean saucepan and stir in the sugar. Place over medium-high heat and bring the liquid to a boil. Cook, uncovered, until the liquid is syrupy, about 30 minutes. Remove from the heat and set aside to cool to room temperature.

Use immediately, or pour into a clean, dry bottle or jar, cover tightly, and refrigerate indefinitely.

Makes about 3½ cups

SIMPLE SUGAR SYRUP

2 cups sugar
2 cups water

In a saucepan, combine the sugar and water. Place over medium-high heat and bring to a boil, stirring occasionally until the sugar is dissolved. Continue cooking, without stirring, until the mixture is clear and the consistency of a light syrup, about 5 minutes longer. Remove from the heat and let cool to room temperature.

Use immediately, or pour into a clean, dry bottle or jar, cover tightly, and refrigerate indefinitely.

Makes about 2¾ cups

VARIATION
Palm-Sugar Syrup. Use 2 cups palm sugar in place of the granulated sugar in the basic recipe and use only 1 cup water. Coarsely chop 2 fresh or thawed frozen screwpine (*pandan*) leaves and add them to the mixture before boiling, or stir a few drops of *pandan* essence into the finished syrup. Strain before using or storing.

KING CHUAM
Thai

GINGER SYRUP

*U*se for Ginger Drinks (page 10), or to sweeten Limeade (page 10) or American-style iced tea. The throat-tingling syrup can also be used to flavor a bowl of summer berries, as a topping for ice cream, or to soak dry cakes. ◗

153

NAHM CHUAM
Thai

SIMPLE SUGAR SYRUP

*U*se this syrup to sweeten Frozen Coconut Cream (page 135), Limeade (page 10), Thai Iced Tea (page 12) or Thai Coffee (page 15), as well as to sweeten other beverages and fresh fruits. ◗

YAM TAENG KWA
Thai

CUCUMBER RELISH

This condiment offers a cooling contrast to the spicy dishes of Thailand and is traditionally served with fried foods. Although the sweet-sour dressing can be made well in advance, toss it with the cucumber only a short time before serving to keep the vegetable crisp and fresh tasting. ❧

154

KING DONG
Thai

PICKLED GINGER

Immature ginger, which has soft flesh and translucent cream-colored skin, is ideal for pickling. If you use mature brown-skinned ginger, be certain that the tuber has not dried out and is unblemished. ❧

CUCUMBER RELISH

¼ cup distilled white vinegar
¼ cup water
¼ cup sugar
¼ teaspoon salt
1 cup thinly sliced seedless (English or hothouse) cucumber or peeled, halved
    and seeded regular cucumber
3 tablespoons thinly sliced red onion half rings
1 teaspoon minced fresh red hot chile
1 tablespoon finely chopped unsalted dry-roasted peanuts
Fresh cilantro (coriander) leaves for garnish

In a small saucepan, combine the vinegar, water, sugar, and salt. Place over medium heat and bring to a boil, stirring until the sugar and salt dissolve. Remove from the heat and let cool to room temperature.

A few minutes before serving, add the cucumber, onion, and chile to the cooled vinegar mixture and toss well. Divide among 4 small dishes. Sprinkle each serving with peanuts, garnish with cilantro leaves, and serve immediately.

Makes 4 condiment-sized servings.

PICKLED GINGER

2 pounds fresh ginger, preferably immature
About 1 quart boiling water
2 cups distilled white vinegar
1 cup sugar
1 tablespoon salt

Peel the ginger. Using a slicer or sharp knife, cut the ginger across the grain into paper-thin slices. Place the slices in a bowl, add the boiling water to cover, and let stand about 2 minutes, then drain in a colander. Transfer the drained ginger to a sterilized glass jar.

In a saucepan, combine the vinegar, sugar, and salt. Place over medium-high heat and bring to a boil, stirring to dissolve the sugar. Remove from the heat and pour over the ginger to cover completely.

Let cool to room temperature, then cover tightly and refrigerate for at least 2 weeks before using or for up to 6 months.

Makes about 1 quart.

PICKLED GARLIC

About 10 young garlic heads, or about 5 mature garlic heads
6 cups water
1½ cups distilled white vinegar
1½ cups sugar
4½ teaspoons salt

If using freshly dug young garlic, wash the heads under cold running water to remove all traces of soil. Without cutting into the cloves, cut off and discard the stems and roots; set aside. If using mature garlic, separate the heads into unpeeled cloves; set aside.

In a large pot, bring the water to a boil over high heat. Add the garlic, reduce the heat to low, and simmer for 10 minutes. Drain in a colander. Pat the garlic dry with paper toweling, then place it in a sterilized glass jar.

In a saucepan, combine the vinegar, sugar, and salt. Place over medium-high heat and bring to a boil, stirring to dissolve the sugar. Remove from the heat and pour over the garlic to cover completely.

Let cool to room temperature, then cover tightly and refrigerate for at least 2 weeks before using or for up to 6 months.

Remove the garlic from the pickling solution and peel them just before serving or using as directed in a recipe.

Makes about 1 quart.

NOTE: To preserve a large quantity of garlic for longer storage, pack the garlic into sterilized jars and pour the vinegar solution over to cover, leaving about ¾-inch headspace between the liquid and the jar rim. Seal and process in a boiling-water bath for 25 minutes, following canning-jar manufacturer's directions. Check the jars and store those with good seals in a cool, dark place for up to 1 year. Any jar that does not have a proper seal should be refrigerated as above.

GRATIEM DONG
Thai

PICKLED GARLIC

*A*lthough commercially pickled garlic bulbs are available in Asian markets, like most good things to eat, those made at home taste best. Whenever possible, choose freshly dug small bulbs for pickling. If only larger garlic bulbs are available, separate the heads into individual cloves for pickling.

155

I've called for the use of pickled garlic in several recipes, including Ginger Salad (page 62) and Rice Porridge (page 20). It also makes a sensational addition to Western-style salads and is an unusual condiment for everything from burgers to grilled fish. ❧

BASICS

ASAM
···
Indonesian and Malaysian

ME CHUA
···
Vietnamese

NAHM MAKAHM BIAK
···
Thai

TAMARIND LIQUID

Tamarind may be purchased in Asian or Spanish markets as packaged blocks of pulp or as whole pods. Bottled liquid concentrate is also available, but lacks the flavor of the other forms. Freshly squeezed lime juice makes a fair substitute. ❧

KAI JIOW
···
Thai

DADAR
···
Indonesian and Malaysian

OMELET STRIPS

Strips of plain omelet are used at room temperature throughout Southeast Asia as a garnish. ❧

TAMARIND LIQUID

1 ounce preserved tamarind pulp (a piece about 2 inches by 1 inch by ½ inch), or 6 ripe tamarind pods
½ cup hot water

If using tamarind pulp, cut the pulp into ½-inch pieces. If using pods, crack them in two and scrape out the pulp.

Place the pulp in a small bowl and add the hot water. Let stand until the pulp is soft, 20 to 30 minutes, occasionally using your fingers to break up and dissolve the pulp. Strain through a fine-mesh sieve into a small bowl, using a spoon to press the pulp against the sides to release all of the liquid. Scrape the pulp that clings to the bottom of the sieve into the bowl with the liquid; discard the fibrous pulp and seeds that remain in the sieve.

Use immediately, or cover tightly and refrigerate for no longer than 24 hours.

Makes about ½ cup.

OMELET STRIPS

3 eggs
Salt
Freshly ground black pepper
1 tablespoon canola oil or other high-quality vegetable oil

In a bowl, beat the eggs with a fork until well blended. Season to taste with salt and pepper.

In a wok or 9- or 10-inch nonstick skillet, heat the oil over medium heat. Pour in the beaten eggs, tilting the pan to spread them into an even layer. Cook until the eggs are set around the edges, about 2 minutes. Using a spatula, gently lift the edges of the omelet and tilt the pan to allow any uncooked egg to run down under the bottom. Continue cooking until the eggs have almost set on top, about 1 minute. Carefully flip the omelet over in the pan and cook just until the bottom is set, about 1 minute longer.

Turn the omelet out onto a clean cloth towel to cool completely. Then tightly roll up the omelet jelly-roll fashion, place on a cutting board, and slice crosswise to make long thin strips. Use as directed in individual recipes.

Makes about 1½ cups.

FRIED SHALLOT

Canola oil or other high-quality vegetable oil for deep-frying
2 cups thinly sliced shallot, separated into rings

In a wok, deep-fat fryer, or large deep pan such as a dutch oven, pour in oil to a depth of 2 inches. Heat to 325° F, or until a single slice of the shallot sizzles just as soon as it is dropped into the hot oil.

Carefully add the shallot to the hot oil and cook until golden, 5 to 10 minutes, depending upon the size of the slices; do not allow to burn. Using a slotted utensil, transfer to paper toweling to drain well and cool.

Use immediately, or store in an airtight container in a cool, dry place for up to 1 week.

Makes about 1⅔ cups.

COCONUT-PEANUT SPRINKLE

2 teaspoons Tamarind Liquid (page 156)
Canola oil or other high-quality vegetable oil for brushing
1 cup grated fresh or dried coconut, preferably unsweetened
½ cup finely chopped shallot
2 teaspoons minced fresh ginger
½ teaspoon minced garlic
1½ teaspoons palm sugar
1 cup coarsely chopped unsalted dry-roasted peanuts
Salt

Prepare the Tamarind Liquid and set aside.

Brush the bottom of a wok, sauté pan, or heavy skillet with oil and place over medium heat. Add the coconut, shallot, ginger, garlic, and sugar and gently toss to blend. Stir in the reserved Tamarind Liquid and cook, stirring and tossing frequently, until the mixture is dry and the coconut is toasted to a golden hue, about 15 minutes if using dried coconut, or about 25 minutes if using fresh coconut. Watch carefully near the end of toasting to avoid burning. Transfer to a bowl and set aside to cool.

Add the peanuts to the cooled coconut mixture, sprinkle with salt to taste, and stir to mix thoroughly. Use immediately, or store in an airtight container at room temperature for up to 3 days.

Makes about 1½ cups.

HOHM LEK JIOW
Thai

BAWANG MERAH GORENG
Indonesian and Malaysian

FRIED SHALLOT

Garlic or red, yellow, or white onions can be used in place of the shallot. No matter which member of the onion family you choose, try to maintain an even thickness in slices for consistency in frying. If cooking garlic, fry over low heat and do not let it get too dark, to prevent bitterness. ◗

157

SERUNDENG
Indonesian

COCONUT-PEANUT SPRINKLE

Offer this typically Indonesian mix for sprinkling over any Southeast Asian curry or other complementary dish. ◗

BASICS

IKAN TERI KAGANG
...
Indonesian

IKAN BILIS
...
Malaysian

CRISPY ANCHOVIES WITH PEANUTS

This crunchy mixture is served in Malaysia with Coconut Rice (page 18) as a popular breakfast dish. On this side of the Pacific, it would make a tasty cocktail snack. ❧

1 cup small dried anchovies (*ikan bilis*)
Canola oil or other high-quality vegetable oil for deep-frying
1 cup unsalted dry-roasted peanuts
Salt
Freshly ground black pepper
About 1 teaspoon sugar

In a colander, thoroughly rinse the fish under cold running water. Remove and discard the heads, if desired. Pat dry with paper toweling and set aside to dry completely, about 30 minutes.

In a wok, deep-fat fryer, or large, deep pan such as a dutch oven, pour in oil to a depth of 2 inches. Heat to 350° F, or until a small piece of bread dropped into the hot oil turns golden brown within about 45 seconds. Carefully add the anchovies and cook until golden and crisp, about 1 minute. Using a slotted utensil, remove the anchovies to paper toweling to drain.

Return the oil to 350° F. Add the peanuts and cook until fragrant, about 1 minute. Using a slotted utensil, remove to paper toweling to drain.

In a bowl, combine the drained anchovies and peanuts and sprinkle to taste with salt, pepper, and sugar. Transfer to a serving bowl and serve warm or at room temperature, or store in an airtight container at room temperature for up to 3 days.

Makes 2 cups.

RICE NOODLES

Dried rice noodles come in varying sizes and most are labeled rice sticks. For tucking into spring rolls or other roll ups, choose very thin, wiry noodles, often labeled rice vermicelli. For soups, salads, or stir-fried dishes, choose flat noodles that are at least ⅛ inch wide.

Dried rice noodles (use amount given for each recipe)

Place the noodles in a bowl, add warm water to cover, and let stand, stirring occasionally, until softened but still firm to the bite, about 15 minutes for very thin noodles, or 30 to 45 minutes for wider noodles. If noodles will be used in a soup or stir-fry, make sure that they are still quite firm to the bite, as they will cook further in the finished dish. Drain in a colander set in a sink and rinse thoroughly with cold running water to remove surface starch.

If noodles will be added to a soup or stir-fry, immerse the rinsed noodles in a bowl of cold water to prevent them from clumping together and set aside. Drain the prepared noodles well just before using as directed in recipes.

If noodles will be used in roll ups or salads, bring 2 to 4 quarts water to a rapid boil over high heat. Drain the noodles, drop into the boiling water, and cook, stirring frequently to prevent the strands from sticking together, until tender yet still firm to the bite, 1 to 2 minutes. Drain and immerse in a bowl of cold water to prevent the noodles from clumping together. If they will be used as a filling for spring rolls or other roll ups, using scissors, cut noodles into pieces about 1 inch long. Drain the prepared noodles well just before using as directed in recipes.

USING FRESH NOODLES

You will need about twice the weight given for dried noodles in recipes. To ready them, cover with boiling water and let stand, stirring occasionally, until strands can be separated and are tender yet still firm to the bite. Drain, rinse, and immerse or cook as directed for dried noodles.

FRIED NOODLE VARIATION

As bases for *sate* or other cooked meats, or as toppings for salads and soups, break very thin, wiry dried noodles into small pieces and drop by small handfuls into hot oil. They will puff up and turn lightly golden and crisp within 12 to 15 seconds. Transfer to a wire rack or paper toweling to drain well.

BASICS

BUN OR BAHN PHO
• • •
Vietnamese

KWAYTIOW
• • •
Thai

LAKSA
• • •
Indonesian and Malaysian

RICE NOODLES

Most North American cooks must rely on dried rice noodles, which I've called for in my recipes. If you have access, however, to a market that caters to an Asian community, look for the daily offerings of fresh rice noodles in varying widths or wide sheets of rice-flour dough for cutting into noodles at home. If you wish to make your own fresh rice noodles, see my recipe in James McNair's Pasta Cookbook. ❧

159

SHOPPING GUIDE

Some of the essential ingredients for Southeast Asian cooking are not commonly found in Western kitchens. Since a few may even prove befuddling at first, a brief introduction to many of them follows. I urge you to search out the authentic ingredients in order to achieve proper flavors.

With the emergence of interest in the cooking of the region, some supermarkets now stock many of the items called for in my recipes or can order them for you. Most of the items are available in markets from coast to coast that cater to Asian communities. If you haven't noticed such ethnic markets in your area, ask owners of a nearby Southeast Asian restaurant where they buy ingredients or look in the yellow pages. Stock up on staples whenever you locate a market nearby or during your travels.

Here I have listed only those ingredients that are used in more than one recipe. If an ingredient is used only once, I have discussed it in the introduction to that particular recipe. To assist you in reading labels, names appear in Indonesian, Malaysian, Thai, and Vietnamese, since most of these products are imported from those nations or those are the names used for fresh products grown locally for Southeast Asian communities. Spellings may differ slightly between brands and suppliers.

Although the flavor will only approximate the intended original taste, I've listed acceptable substitutes whenever possible.

ASIAN BASIL (Indonesian and Malaysian *kemangi*, Thai *bai*, or Vietnamese *rau que*). Several members of the basil family are preferred by Southeast Asians over the familiar sweet basil (*Ocinum basilicum*) identified with Italian cooking. Most popular and easiest to find in the produce section of Asian markets is a cultivar of *O. basilicum*, often sold as Thai basil and known as *bai horapah* in Thai and *rau huyng* in Vietnamese, with small leaves, purple stems, and a subtle licorice taste. Also look for peppery, fragrant, and purple-tinged "holy" basil (*O. sanctum*), or *bai graprao* in Thai, as well as the small-leafed lemon basil (*O. carnum*), or *bai maengluk* in Thai, sometimes referred to as bush or Greek basil. All basil varieties are easily grown from seeds or nursery seedlings in a sunny garden or in pots in full sun. Please do not use the flavorless dried form. *Substitute:* any fresh basil variety.

BANANA LEAVES (Thai *bai gluay* or Vietnamese *la chuoi*). Huge leaves of banana palms (*Musa* species), used as wrappers for steamed or grilled fare, are frequently available frozen, usually from the Philippines. Some florists sell fresh leaves, but these leaves have most likely been sprayed with toxic chemicals and should not be used. Banana trees are also easy to grow indoors and in mild climates. *Substitute:* ti leaves, fresh corn husks, aluminum foil, or parchment paper.

BEAN SAUCE (Chinese *jiang* or Thai *dao jiow*). Made from salted, fermented soybeans, this light brown Chinese staple is variously labeled brown bean sauce, yellow bean sauce, soybean sauce, or bean paste. The whole bean form is less salty and more flavorful than the ground version. *Substitute:* less salty and thinner Vietnamese soybean sauce (*tuong*).

CANDLENUTS (Indonesian *kemiri* or *tingkih* or Malaysian *buah keras*). Round, oily, beige nuts of the candlenut tree (*Aleurites moluccana*), known in Hawaii as *kukui*, are imported in packages and are pulverized to add texture to dishes. Shelled nuts must be cooked before eating. *Substitute:* raw Brazil or macadamia nuts, cashews, or blanched almonds.

CHILES (Indonesian *cabe* or *lombok*, Malaysian *cabai* or *cili*, Thai *prik*, or Vietnamese *ot*). Introduced to the region by Portuguese sailors, chiles have become a major component of Southeast Asian cookery. Most popular are the tiny bird or bird's-eye variety (*Capsicum frutenscens*), often sold as Thai chiles or *prik kii noo*, *cabe rawit* in Indonesian, and *cili padi* in Malaysian. Any hot chile, including serrano or jalapeño, may be used in their place; vary the amount to taste according to the heat of the chile. All fresh chiles are sold either in their green state or ripened to various shades of yellow, orange, or red. Whole fresh chiles freeze well, so I stock up on red ones whenever I find them. Red chiles are also available dried and are often soaked in hot water to soften before using. *Substitute:* bottled chile sauce, ground dried chile, or dried chile flakes.

CHILE SAUCE (Indonesian and Malaysian *sambal ulek* and *sambal bajak* or Vietnamese *tuong ot*). *Sambal ulek* and *tuong ot* are made from ground fresh red hot chiles packed in vinegar or tamarind liquid and salt. *Sambal bajak* is prepared from cooked chiles seasoned with shallot and spices. Both products may be labeled chile sauce or chile paste. Quality varies greatly, so you may need to sample a few to discover brands you prefer. *Substitute:* recipes on pages 148-149 or Chinese chile sauces or pastes from Sichuan.

CHILE-GARLIC SAUCE (Vietnamese *tuong ot toi*). Similar to *tuong ot* discussed in the preceding entry, but with the addition of garlic. *Substitute:* chile-garlic sauces or pastes from China.

COCONUT MILK (Indonesian or Malaysian *santan*, Thai *nahm ga-ti*, or Vietnamese *nuoc dua*). This is not the juice inside a whole coconut or the sweetened canned product sold as cream of coconut used for making tropical drinks. It is instead the rich, unsweetened extraction of the grated nut of the coconut palm (*Cocos nucifera*). Make your own from freshly grated or unsweetened dried coconut (recipe on page 140) or purchase canned, which is far easier, richer, and thicker than homemade. Flavor varies with brand, so you may need to try several to find one you prefer. Sometimes available frozen, usually from the Philippines. Coconut cream rises to the top of coconut milk and can be easily scooped off. *No substitute.*

CURRY PASTE (Thai *krueng gaeng*). Various mixtures of herbs and spices ground into a paste and cooked briefly before adding to curries and many other dishes. Although freshly made pastes (pages 142-145) have much better flavor, canned pastes from Thailand are convenient. **No substitute.**

DRIED SHRIMP (Indonesian and Malaysian *udang kering*, Thai *goong haeng*, or Vietnamese *tom kho*). Shelled, dried, and salted shrimp are used throughout Southeast Asia to add flavor to numerous dishes. Use soon after opening packages, as they turn rancid very quickly. It's best to keep them in the freezer after purchasing and to use within a month. The shrimp can be used as they are, soaked in hot water to soften before using as directed in recipes, or ground in a spice grinder, blender, or heavy mortar with a pestle to use as a condiment for sprinkling. Also sold in ground form, sometimes labeled dried shrimp powder. **No substitute.**

FISH SAUCE (Thai *nahm plah* or Vietnamese *nuoc man*). Basic to all cuisines of Southeast Asia, this thin, brown, extremely nutritious sauce, made from brined anchovies that are fermented under the blazing sun, is used to add saltiness and flavor. Fortunately, the flavor is far better than the strong aroma and you'll quickly become accustomed or even addicted. Clear amber liquid, generally sold at a higher price, indicates that the sauce was taken from the top of the barrel and is valued as a table condiment or dipping sauce component; darker versions result from later siphoning and are usually reserved for cooking. Produced throughout Southeast Asia and China, although Vietnamese and Thai products are considered the finest. *Substitute:* light soy sauce combined with salt.

GALANGA (Indonesian *laos*, Malaysian *lengkuas*, Thai *kah*, or Vietnamese *rieng*). This rhizome of a *Zingiber* species is also spelled *galangal* and *galingale*, and is sometimes called Java root or Siamese ginger. The skin is lighter than ginger and is marked with stripes and there are often pink shoots. Its texture is tougher and its flavor is more citruslike but less flavorful than its familiar ginger cousin. Although fresh is preferable, frozen is adequate. Avoid flavorless dried or powdered forms. Always used in cooked dishes, and never eaten raw. *Substitute:* fresh ginger.

JASMINE ESSENCE (Thai *mali* or Vietnamese *nuoc hoa*). Concentrated extract of jasmine blossoms is sold in small bottles for adding sparingly

to sweets. Distilled jasmine water is also available, but more of it is needed to equal the flavor of extract. **Substitute:** banana essence or rose- or orange-flower water or extract.

KAFFIR LIME LEAVES (Indonesian *duan jeruk purut*, Malaysian *daun limau purut*, or Thai *bai makroot*). Leaves of the wild lime tree (*Citrus hystrix*) are extremely fragrant, almost perfumelike, and grow in attached pairs. They are most often available frozen, but occasionally fresh. Dried leaves bear little resemblance to the fresh and are not recommended. *Substitute:* fresh pesticide-free domestic lime or lemon leaves or an equal portion of freshly grated lime zest moistened with a little lime juice.

LEMONGRASS (Indonesian and Malaysian *serai*, Thai *takrai*, or Vietnamese *xa*). This clumpy grass (*Cymbopogon citratus*) with a distinctive lemony aroma and flavor is also known as citronella. Fresh stalks are now becoming more readily available in supermarkets and plants are easy to grow in warm, sunny gardens or pots. To prepare for cooking, cut off and discard the tough root end and green grass top, then use only the tender, inner white portion. Dried or powdered forms have little flavor and should be left on the grocer's rack. *Substitute:* equal portion of grated or minced fresh lemon zest moistened with a little fresh lemon juice.

MUNG BEAN NOODLES (Indonesian *sotanghoon*, Malaysian *tunghoon*, or Thai *woon sen*). These thin noodles, usually imported from China or Taiwan and labeled *sai fun*, are made from mung bean flour and become clear when reconstituted by soaking in hot water. Various English labels include cellophane, bean thread, and glass noodles and long rice. *No substitute.*

PALM SUGAR (Indonesian *gula Jawa* or *gula Merah*, Malaysian *gula Malacca*, or Thai *nahm tahn beep* or *nahm tahn maprao*). This ages-old sweetener is extracted from the sap of several species of palm trees, including the areng palm (*Arenga saccharifera*), palmyra palm (*Borassus flabellifer*), and coconut palm (*Cocos nucifera*). Sugar color varies from pale tan to dark brown and the texture ranges from hard grainy blocks to a spoonable gooey paste of palm sugar and water in jars or cans. Also may be labeled coconut sugar, coconut candy, Java sugar, or palm sugar *jaggery* from India. This is not date sugar made from date palms and sold in natural-food stores. *Substitute:* maple sugar or brown sugar blended with a little maple syrup to moisten.

PANDAN ESSENCE The deep green extract of screwpine leaves (see following entry) is sold in small bottles, usually imported from Indonesia or the Netherlands, for use as a substitute for whole leaves. **Substitute:** Screwpine leaves.

RICE PAPER WRAPPERS (Vietnamese *bahn trang*). Tissue thin, very brittle disks or wedges, made from rice flour, are sold dried in various sizes and must be soaked in water to soften before using. *Substitute:* freshly made thin crêpes or pancakes.

SCREWPINE LEAVES. (Indonesian and Malaysian *pandan* or Thai *bai toey hom*). Long, narrow leaves of the screwpine (*Pandanus odoratissimus*) are used to add a grassy-to-nutty flavor and a green tint to rice, sweets, and other dishes. To release more flavor, scrape the leaves with the tines of a fork or chop them before using. *Substitute: pandan* essence; use sparingly.

SHALLOTS (Indonesian and Malaysian *bawang merah* or Thai *hom daeng* or *hom lek*). Throughout Southeast Asia, these small bulbs (*Allium ascalonicum*) with purple-red-tinted flesh covered with caramel papery skin are known as Bombay onions and are the region's choice member of the onion family. Shallots are available in most supermarkets. *Substitute:* red Spanish onions.

SHRIMP PASTE (Indonesian *trasi,* Malaysian *blachan* or *belaccan,* or Thai *ga-pi*). Look for this potently aromatic paste made from ground fermented shrimp in two types: bottled moist paste from Thailand, or less potent versions from China, and firm dried bricks from Indonesia and Malaysia. Don't be turned off by the strong aroma; the unique flavor that the paste adds to finished dishes is far better than the initial smell. *Substitute:* anchovy paste, ground presoaked dried shrimp, or thin Vietnamese shrimp sauce (*mam tom* or *mam ruoc).*

SOY SAUCE (Indonesian *kecap*, Malaysian *kechap soya*, Thai *si-yu,* or Vietnamese *si dau*). Although fish sauce is more commonly used to add saltiness and flavor throughout Southeast Asia, many dishes also call for soy sauce, the familiar liquid extracted from cooked, fermented, and salted soybeans, to add both flavor and color. Chinese-style soy sauce is produced for and by Chinese communities throughout Southeast Asia in both light and dark styles. Light soy sauce is thin and used in dishes where a delicate flavor is preferred; Japanese soy sauce (*shoyu*) is a light soy sauce that is generally less salty and a bit sweeter than its Chinese counterparts and was used in developing my recipes, unless otherwise specified. Dark soy sauce is aged longer, then mixed with molasses for a hint of sweetness and a deep, rich hue, although not as sweet as Javanese sweet soy sauce (see following entry). **No substitute.**

SWEET SOY SAUCE (Indonesian *kecap manis*). A mixture of dark soy sauce and palm sugar from Java that adds richness, thickness, sweetness, and color to cooked dishes. The sauce may also contain galanga, garlic, aromatic *salam* leaves, and star anise and is the common table condiment of Indonesia. *Substitute:* See recipe on page 149.

INDEX TO SOUTHEAST ASIAN RECIPES IN OTHER JAMES McNAIR COOKBOOKS

RECIPE INDEX

165

TABLE OF EQUIVALENTS

The exact equivalents in the following tables have been rounded for convenience.

❧

US/UK

oz = ounce
lb = pound
in = inch
ft = foot
tbl = tablespoon
fl oz = fluid ounce
qt = quart

METRIC

g = gram
kg = kilogram
mm = millimeter
cm = centimeter
ml = milliliter
l = liter

WEIGHTS

US/UK	Metric
1 oz	30 g
2 oz	60 g
3 oz	90 g
4 oz (¼ lb)	125 g
5 oz (⅓ lb)	155 g
6 oz	185 g
7 oz	220 g
8 oz (½ lb)	250 g
10 oz	315 g
12 oz (¾ lb)	75 g
14 oz	40 g
16 oz (1 lb)	500 g
1 ½ lb	750 g
2 lb	1 kg
3 lb	1.5 kg

OVEN TEMPERATURES

Fahrenheit	Celsius	Gas
250	120	½
275	140	1
300	150	2
325	160	3
350	180	4
375	190	5
400	200	6
425	220	7
450	230	8
475	240	9
500	260	10

LIQUIDS

US	Metric	UK
2 tbl	30 ml	1 fl oz
¼ cup	60 ml	2 fl oz
⅓ cup	80 ml	3 fl oz
½ cup	125 ml	4 fl oz
⅔ cup	60 ml	5 fl oz
¾ cup	180 ml	6 fl oz
1 cup	250 ml	8 fl oz
1 ½ cups	375 ml	12 fl oz
2 cups	500 ml	16 fl oz
4 cups/1 qt	1 l	32 fl oz

LENGTH MEASURES

⅛ in	3 mm
¼ in	6 mm
½ in	12 mm
1 in	2.5 cm
2 in	5 cm
3 in	7.5 cm
4 in	10 cm
5 in	13 cm
6 in	15 cm
7 in	18 cm
8 in	20 cm
9 in	23 cm
10 in	25 cm
11 in	28 cm
12 in/1 ft	30 cm

Equivalents for Commonly Used Ingredients

All-Purpose (Plain) Flour/Rice Flour

¼ cup	1 oz	30 g
⅓ cup	1 ½ oz	45 g
½ cup	2 oz	60 g
¾ cup	3 oz	90 g
1 cup	4 oz	125 g
1 ½ cups	6 oz	185 g
2 cups	8 oz	250 g

Semolina

¼ cup	1 oz	30 g
⅓ cup	2 oz	60 g
½ cup	3 c	90 g
¾ cup		125 g
1 cup		155 g

Rice

⅓ cup	2 oz	60 g
½ cup	2 ½ oz	75 g
¾ cup	4 oz	125 g
1 cup	5 oz	155 g
1 ½ cups	8 oz	250 g

Dried Beans

¼ cup	1 ½ oz	45 g
⅓ cup	2 oz	60 g
½ cup	3 oz	90 g
¾ cup	5 oz	155 g
1 cup	6 oz	185 g
1 ¼ cups	8 oz	250 g
1 ½ cups	12 oz	375 g

Palm Sugar (moist bottled type)

¼ cup	3 oz	90 g
½ cup	6 oz	185 g
1 cup	12 oz	375 g

Brown Sugar

¼ cup	1½ oz	45 g
½ cup	3 oz	90 g
1 cup	5½ oz	170 g

ACKNOWLEDGMENTS

Walter R. Allen

John Carr

Chris and Bob Cook

Gretchen Eichinger

Jan Ellis

Maile and Mark Forbert

Carol Gallagher

Ethan Halm

Louis Hicks

Gail High

Steven Holden

Hank Julian

Marian May

Meri McEneny

Lucille and J.O. McNair

Martha McNair

Sandra and Jim Moore

Shellie and Richard Moore

John Nyquist

Peter Olsen

Jack Porter

John Richardson

Nancy and Tom Riess

Julie Schaper

Michele Sordi

Kristi Spence

Gregory Taylor

Sara and Brad Timpson

Barry Wolpa

To the multitalented staff of Chronicle Books, as we celebrate this twenty-fifth book and tenth anniversary of working together, for their ongoing efforts in my behalf. Very special thanks to Jack Jensen, my supportive publisher, and to Bill LeBlond, my patient editor, for their friendship through all of these books and for allowing me to find and express my creativity with each volume. Special thanks to hard-working yet ever-cheerful Leslie Jonath and Brenda Rae Eno for their great work on my books.

To Sharon Silva, copy editor, for continuing to turn my ideas and words into more readable language.

To Southeast Asian food authorities Rosslyn Bartlett and Nancie McDermott for sharing their expertise.

To Rick Dinihanian and John Lyle of Green Lizard Design for putting my words and pictures together in a layout that expresses their sensitive graphic style. It's a wonderful experience to collaborate with good friends.

To Iris Fuller of Fillamento and her fabulous staff for loaning so many of the props shown in my photographs. And to Antonia Allegra and Grant Showley for loaning items from their own collections.

To Alan May for the resplendent author's portrait and to Michael Duté for the enchanting title page painting.

To the recipe testers listed alongside for cooking my dishes at home on their own and returning helpful feedback.

To my family and friends for being there whenever I need their assistance or encouragement. As always, special thanks to my sister, Martha, and her family, John, Devereux, and Ryan, for numerous kindnesses. And much gratitude to Peter Baumgartner and John Carr for sharing their city homes during my early research and shopping expeditions.

To Beauregard Ezekiel Valentine, Joshua J. Chew, Michael T. Wigglebutt, Miss Vivien "Bunny" Fleigh, and Miss Olivia de Pusspuss for lapping up all the leftover coconut milk and offering their tail-wagging compliments to my cooking.

And to Andrew Moore, my devoted partner in life and work, for his creative and invaluable contributions to our homes, offices, and books. He deserves to share equal credit with me on the writing and with the editors on the editing of this volume.